"Deep in the Reformation worship traditi[on] ... consistent use of the Aaronic blessing. So it i[s ...] recommend Michael Glodo's book-length tre[atment of this] portion of God's word, deepening our understanding and renewing our use of our Reformed heritage."

Bryan Chapell, Stated Clerk, Presbyterian Church in America

"This book infuses our shallow understanding of what it means to be blessed with scriptural insight and textual richness. It invites us to think more deeply about what is promised in the familiar words of the Aaronic blessing so that we hear them with fresh meaning and find ourselves receiving them with profound joy."

Nancy Guthrie, author, *Blessed: Experiencing the Promise of the Book of Revelation*

"Michael Glodo's *The Lord Bless You and Keep You* is a rich exposition of a beloved and important divine blessing. Glodo's many years of teaching biblical studies and pastoral theology, as well as his own pastoral experience and instincts, really show up in this book. This exegetical, biblical-theological deep dive into the Aaronic blessing will edify you devotionally and equip you to understand the profundity of what it means for the Lord's face to shine upon his people."

Ligon Duncan, Chancellor and CEO, Reformed Theological Seminary

"We often hear the words of the Aaronic blessing pronounced at the end of worship services. There's a beauty to its rhythm; its vocabulary sparkles with grace—*bless, keep, peace*. And we all want God's face to shine on us! And yet, despite the popularity of this blessing, we rarely hear anyone explaining what these words really mean or what difference they make to daily life. Thankfully, Michael Glodo has arrived to help us! Combining the heart of a pastor with the understanding of an Old Testament scholar, as well as a deep appreciation of worship, he brings us treasure in both hands. *The Lord Bless You and Keep You* is a book to savor and enjoy."

Sinclair B. Ferguson, Chancellor's Professor of Systematic Theology, Reformed Theological Seminary; Teaching Fellow, Ligonier Ministries

"The Aaronic blessing is one of the great poems of the Bible, yet its simple language can catch us off guard. We find ourselves so familiar with it that we take its content for granted and miss its striking depths. Michael Glodo has done us a big service in this little book on the brief blessing that carries such great truths—in particular great truths about faces, both ours and God's—truths many of us were not ready to appreciate until we spent months covering our faces in public. Far from being irrelevant today, this ancient blessing is, in fact, all the more true and precious to those who profess Jesus as Lord. Learn what it means and pray it afresh over the souls of those you love most."

David Mathis, Senior Teacher and Executive Editor, desiringGod.org; Pastor, Cities Church, Saint Paul, Minnesota; author, *Habits of Grace*

"The Aaronic blessing (Numbers 6) is often the great blessing offered to God's people before they depart from worship services and scatter into the world. These words have surely been some of the most familiar among God's people for millennia. Yet few have thought about their importance. Michael Glodo not only defines and provides insight into these lines but also demonstrates the great influence the Aaronic blessing has on the entire Christian life. Be prepared to experience an old text in a new way and have your eyes opened to a life lived in light of the Aaronic blessing. The comfort, challenge, and grace this knowledge provides will bring a new appreciation for the beauty of our God and his blessings upon his people."

Jason Helopoulos, Senior Pastor, University Reformed Church, East Lansing, Michigan; author, *The New Pastor's Handbook* and *Covenantal Baptism*

"In this book, Michael Glodo offers more than just a wonderful study of the Aaronic blessing. He provides a rich biblical-theological survey of the theme of God's 'face' as it unfolds across the pages of Scripture and wise pastoral-theological applications of the numerous ways God 'shines' his face on us in our public worship and in our day-to-day lives."

Scott Swain, President and Professor of Systematic Theology, Reformed Theological Seminary, Orlando

"I have pronounced the Aaronic blessing over God's people hundreds of times over four decades of pastoral ministry. Thanks to Michael Glodo's book—with his outstanding exposition of Numbers 6:22–27, his theological and pastoral insights, and his sound liturgical advice—I'll forever pronounce the benediction with much greater conviction, meaning, and joy. Whether we pronounce or receive God's blessing, this book is really worth reading."

Sandy Willson, Pastor Emeritus, Second Presbyterian Church, Memphis, Tennessee

"My earliest memory of church is the pronouncement of the Aaronic blessing at the close of worship. It seemed to connect us with ancient Israel and with the church through the ages, militant and triumphant. Michael Glodo has written a beautiful book that captures the emotional, theological, liturgical, and spiritual depths of this word from God. It will edify and strengthen you in faith and hope. It is the product of love for the church to the glory of God."

Liam Goligher, Senior Minister, Tenth Presbyterian Church, Philadelphia, Pennsylvania

The Lord Bless You and Keep You

The Lord Bless You and Keep You

The Promise of the Gospel in the Aaronic Blessing

Michael J. Glodo

WHEATON, ILLINOIS

Library of Congress Cataloging-in-Publication Data

Names: Glodo, Michael J., 1958- author.
Title: The Lord bless you and keep you : the promise of the gospel in the aaronic blessing / Michael J. Glodo.
Description: Wheaton, Illinois : Crossway, [2023] | Includes bibliographical references and index.
Identifiers: LCCN 2022054287 (print) | LCCN 2022054288 (ebook) | ISBN 9781433584237 (trade paperback) | ISBN 9781433584244 (pdf) | ISBN 9781433584268 (epub)
Subjects: LCSH: Aaron (Biblical priest) | Benediction—Judaism. | Christianity.
Classification: LCC BS580.A23 G563 2023 (print) | LCC BS580.A23 (ebook) | DDC 296.4/5—dc23/eng/20230419
LC record available at https://lccn.loc.gov/2022054287
LC ebook record available at https://lccn.loc.gov/2022054288

To the Bride and to the Lamb
Revelation 19:7

You have said, "Seek my face."
My heart says to you,
  "Your face, Lord, do I seek."

Contents

Acknowledgments

MY HEARTFELT THANKS to all of the mother kirks, especially Central Presbyterian Church and Sutter Presbyterian Church in the 1980s, Orangewood Presbyterian Church in the 1990s, Knox Presbyterian Church in the 2000s, and St. Paul's Presbyterian Church (Orlando) today, with special gratitude for those under-shepherds who modeled what it is to be a "friend of the bride," JES, AAJ, WMF, SDF, WFM, LED, JTS. God knows who you are.

Thank you as well to those colleagues from whom I have learned so much and who have encouraged the development of this work.

My late colleague Roger Nicole, alluding to the fact that he and Annette had no children but some forty-thousand books, was fond of quipping, "My books are my children." To all my students, current and past, you are my books. Thank you for entrusting a portion of your preparation to me.

Thank you to my wife, Vicki, and children, Rachel and Samuel, for believing the myth of my greatness in spite of my best efforts to debunk it.

Introduction

C. S. LEWIS'S PERSONAL FAVORITE of his own novels, *Till We Have Faces*, is a theodicy—an accusation against the gods. It is told by an aged, veiled queen named Orual who wore a veil her entire life. She did so at first because her father the king thought her ugly—"curd face," he called her when he first told her to cover her face. But as time went on, she found the veil to be a source of power.

> As years passed and there were fewer in the city . . . who remembered my face, the wildest stories got about as to what that veil hid. . . . Some said . . . that it was frightful beyond endurance; a pig's, bear's, cat's or elephant's face. The best story was that I had no face at all; if you stripped off my veil you'd find emptiness. But another sort . . . said that I wore a veil because I was of a beauty so dazzling that if I let it be seen all men in the world would run mad; or else that Ungit [their god] was jealous of my beauty and had promised to blast me if I went bareface. The upshot of all this nonsense was that I became something very mysterious and awful.[1]

1 C. S. Lewis, *Till We Have Faces: A Myth Retold* (New York: HarperOne, 2017), 259–60.

I

While the veil gave Orual power over others, making her mysterious like their gods, she came to realize it also meant a loss of her humanity. Only by removing her veil at the end of the novel did she become fully human again and get the long-sought answer to her questions from the gods.

More than any other physical feature, we associate the face with a person. And while we say "the eyes are the window to the soul," award-winning portrait artist Catherine Prescott has said that the mouth is more important than the eyes. According to Prescott, the mouth is where the face's expression is found because it is part of the soft tissue of the face. While the eyes can indicate six or seven emotions on their own, without the mouth to reinforce what the eyes express, one doesn't know for certain what the eyes are saying. The mouth is more variable and expressive than the eyes. Therefore, Prescott insists it's the mouth that shows whether someone is revealing or hiding themselves or whether someone is hostile or friendly. The point is that to really know someone, we must see the whole face not just the eyes.[2]

Faces matter to people, and so it's not surprising that faces matter in the Bible. Near the very beginning of the biblical story we find Adam and Eve hiding from the face of God (Gen. 3:8). The end of the biblical story finds believers seeing Jesus Christ face-to-face and being like him (1 John 3:2). All

---

2   The beginning of this introduction is adapted from a chapel sermon at Reformed Theological Seminary Orlando in December 2020, which developed into an article-length treatment "We Still Have Faces," *Reformed Faith & Practice* 5, no. 3 (December 2020), 10–19, excerpts of which are included here by permission. "Catherine Prescott on What Is Lost When We Don Face Masks," interview with Ken Myers, Friday Feature, Mars Hill Audio, August 21, 2020, https://marshillaudio.org/pages/heres-what-youre -missing#prescott.

along the way are dramatic encounters with the face of God. In Psalms the face of God is the focus of delights and despair, penance and praise, petitions and punishment. The face of God is a central theme of encounters with and knowing God in the Old Testament. The acme of this theme is the Aaronic blessing, possibly the most-frequently heard passage of Scripture in Christian worship.

The LORD spoke to Moses, saying, "Speak to Aaron and his sons, saying, Thus you shall bless the people of Israel: you shall say to them,

> The LORD bless you and keep you;
> the LORD make his face to shine upon you and be gracious
> to you;
> the LORD lift up his countenance upon you and give you
> peace.

"So shall they put my name upon the people of Israel, and I will bless them." (Num. 6:22–27)

The Aaronic benediction brings us face-to-face with God's gracious gaze. The imagery of God unveiling his face to bless his people is in stark contrast to Orual's mysterious and frightful gods. Yet the Aaronic blessing is not the climax of the story of the Bible. The blessing points forward to the unveiling of God's glory in the face of Jesus Christ (2 Cor. 3:18).

The prominence of God's shining face and its centrality to the new covenant beckon us to reflect deeply on it. Luther called the

Psalms "a little Bible" since each psalm sets out in brief form all that is taught in the rest of Scripture.[3] I am suggesting the same observation is true of the Aaronic blessing. By exploring the blessing's background, central elements, spiritual meaning in Israel, and realization in Christ, we will grasp the comprehensive nature of the theme of God's face and be enabled to stand more fully in its light. We will see that *God made us with faces so that his could shine on ours and that the Aaronic blessing could be to us not only a "little Bible," but a "little gospel."*

Our survey will begin with the background behind the blessing; the history of God's face, if you will. We will consider and look for hints of God's face (and ours) at creation, the fall, Jacob's encounter with God at Peniel, and Moses's vision on Mount Sinai. With that background in view, we'll examine the Aaronic blessing itself in its original context and in its influence on the spiritual life of Israel as traced out in the Psalms. This Old Testament background will equip us to see the scope and substance of the blessing revealed in Jesus Christ, principally in the Gospel of John and 2 Corinthians 3–4. To see God, however, means to be seen by him. Therefore, chapters 4 and 5 will develop our understanding of God's gracious gaze in Christ, first with implications for ourselves and then with implications for how we think and act toward others. Before concluding we will return to the Aaronic blessing itself to reflect on how it can illuminate and animate our worship. Finally an appendix offers a sample order of worship to stimulate ideas for applying this study in corporate worship.

3   Martin Luther, *Word and Sacrament I*, Luther's Works, vol. 35, ed. E. Theodore Bachman (Philadelphia, PA: Muhlenberg, 1960), 254.

The metaphor of God's shining face itself calls for contemplation. This book regularly offers numerous Scripture references and prompts for more in-depth reflection. I invite readers to pause to look up Scripture passages, read them in their context, and reflect. Some readers may wish to keep a journal for their reflections and growing understanding on the prospect of God's gracious gaze on his people.

Each chapter ends with a "For Further Reflection" section. Some of the questions and suggestions assume a group context since, as chapter 5 might suggest, groups are the best places to contemplate the blessings of God's gracious gaze. All of the questions can be applied to individual study with a bit of imagination. If you are studying this book in a group, keep in mind that the chapters are not written in uniform slices like a symmetrically sliced pizza, but more like the movements of a symphony, which differ in character and length but that all contribute to the unity of the single work. Therefore, some chapters may lend themselves to more than one group discussion session.

If any of my children ever passes through Chattanooga, they leap at the chance to heed the barn roof signs for miles around and "see Rock City" again. Even though they have been there many times before as children and adults, they get nostalgic revisiting the familiar nooks and crannies, and they revel in finding new pathways and approaches that put the old sites in a new light. Similarly, this study may be a first visit to the sites of the Aaronic blessing for some of you. To others there may not be many new sites, but perhaps you will find new vistas of the familiar. Whichever the case, cultivating a growing appreciation of God's gaze is a worthy lifelong pursuit. In Psalm 27:8 the psalmist recites an invitation from God: "You have said, 'Seek my face.'" To this invitation we hear the psalmist's resolve: "My heart says to you, 'Your face, LORD, do I seek.'" May this study encourage and enable your search for the beatific vision.

1

The Prequel to the Aaronic Blessing

The Context of the Blessing

SEVERAL YEARS AGO I SAW A MOVIE CLIP at the end of a presentation. The scene depicted an older man in Arlington National Cemetery kneeling before an alabaster cross. "I tried to live my life the best I could. I hope that was enough. I hope at least in your eyes I earned what all of you have done for me."[1] Turning to his approaching wife, he pled with her, "Tell me I've led a good life. Tell me I'm a good man."

It was a poignant scene and made the speaker's point. However, I was left wondering about the surrounding story of the clip since the speaker didn't provide any context. At this point you might assume I don't see many films since that scene is widely known

1   *Saving Private Ryan*, directed by Steven Spielberg (Universal City, CA: DreamWorks Pictures, 1998).

7

as the dramatic conclusion to Steven Spielberg's blockbuster *Saving Private Ryan*, starring Tom Hanks. While I do watch my fair share of films and I had watched most of *Saving Private Ryan* several times before, I had never seen the conclusion!

Previous Encounters

A similar experience can be true of how we often read the Bible. Many individual portions of Scripture are familiar to us, but we don't always know them as part of a larger story and context. This is often true of the story of the Aaronic blessing (Num. 6:24–26). This blessing arises out of a long-running story and leads to the climactic conclusion. The story is that of the "beatific vision," of seeing God:

> One thing have I asked of the LORD,
>   that will I seek after:
> that I may dwell in the house of the LORD
>   all the days of my life,
> to gaze upon the beauty of the LORD
>   and to inquire in his temple . . .
>
> Hear, O LORD, when I cry aloud;
>   be gracious to me and answer me!
> You have said, "Seek my face."
> My heart says to you,
>   "Your face, LORD, do I seek." (Ps. 27:4, 7–8)

The story that precedes the blessing of God's gracious gaze is one of people seeing, avoiding, longing for, and catching a glimpse of the face of God. The face of God is a looming visage across the chapters of the Bible leading to when God would administer this blessing through Aaron. To fully understand the Aaronic blessing, we must appreciate the prequel events that constitute the context of God's gracious gaze. If the Aaronic blessing means that God has made us with faces so that his could shine on ours, we need to know the backstory of faces. We'll find that this context consists of past face-to-face encounters with God. There are four such encounters which will help us, two in Eden and one each at Penuel and Sinai.

God Made Us with Faces

The first mention of God's face occurs when God finds Adam and Eve hiding after their "declaration of independence" by eating the forbidden fruit. Having experienced a loss of original righteousness, their eyes were opened and they perceived that they were naked. Their autonomous move left them without the protection and provision of God's covenant lordship. Consequently, when God drew near for the kind of intimate fellowship with them that had existed before, they hid themselves from God's face (Gen. 3:8). Most Bible translations say "presence" instead of "face," but it is the same Hebrew word (*pāneh*). The anthropomorphic language, such as God "walking," justifies a more literal rendering of "face" though used in a figurative way (3:8). Adam and Eve tried to hide themselves from being seen, from God's face, and from his gaze.

Seeing God and being seen by him in fellowship is the very purpose for which people were created. God made people in his image and likeness in order for them to reflect his glory (Gen. 1:26). Just as a mirror will only reflect light in the presence of that light, to be made in God's image reflects God's purpose for us to be in his presence. To be in God's image was also to be a son of God. The same term "image" is used in Genesis 5:3 to describe Adam's relationship to his son Seth. We might say a particular child is the "spitting image" of a parent. So also to be made in God's image means being in a filial relationship to him. Additionally, "likeness" (Gen. 1:26) denotes a being who is a relational creature. This is because the particular Hebrew word (*děmût*) describes three-dimensional things such as sculptures rather than two-dimensional things such as paintings. Three-dimensional things require perspective in order to be known fully and require others in order to know themselves. If we were two-dimensional creatures, we could know ourselves fully simply by looking in a mirror, but as three-dimensional creatures we need other people to help us see ourselves completely, for example the back of our heads. The sources of our self-knowledge are many. For example, we could ask for direct descriptions of ourselves from our friends. A vast source of self-knowledge is what we learn about ourselves as we move through life and observe the effects (or non-effects) we have on those around us.

Most importantly, we need to be seen and known by God to fully know ourselves. This interpersonal, relational need is the essence of our nature and its satisfaction is found in seeing and being seen by God. God made us with faces so that his could shine on ours.

The Hidden Face of Shame

God instituted curses on the man and woman for their rebellion (Gen. 3:16–19), but they were only symptoms or signs of the greater curse of alienation from God. The curses would serve as painful teachers, and when paired with the promise of redemption (the first gospel or *protoevangelium* of Genesis 3:15), the curses might fuel a longing for restoration with God. The overwhelming and fundamental tragedy of human autonomy was the creature's alienation from God the Creator. The compulsion to hide from God's face meant the loss of protection, provision, and self for our first parents, and shame came to dominate the human condition. From then on people would live with a simultaneous longing and loathing for the face of God, because it was and is both the greatest delight and the greatest horror. The curses of the fall meant life would be futile. God would preserve the life-giving power of the womb and the soil, and yet both would provide perpetual reminders of alienation from the face of God as humanity was driven out of Eden. While God graciously covered their shame in giving them garments (Gen. 3:21), he did not cover their faces. Paradise was lost, but only for a time, for they took with them the promise that "everything sad" would become "untrue" (to paraphrase J. R. R. Tolkien's character, Sam Gamgee). One day a seed of the woman would crush the head of the serpent (Gen. 3:15).

Cain

As the first person born into the world outside of Eden, Cain exemplifies the "fallen face," the face that looks downward instead of toward the face of God. True to the synergism in his name ("I have gotten a man with the help of the Lord," Gen. 4:1), Cain is fundamentally self-reliant, treating God as a totem rather than as the generous Creator and sustainer of life. The difference between his and his younger brother Abel's offerings was not that

Abel's involved blood as is popularly believed, for these were of-ferings not sacrifices. Offerings were not for atonement but were representative portions of what God had graciously provided to them. Cain and Abel each brought a portion of what God had provided through their respective callings as farmer and shepherd. The difference between the offerings was that Abel brought the very best—the fat portions of the firstborn lamb—while Cain brought "an" offering (Gen. 4:3–4). Abel's offering was made in faith; Cain's was a token gesture.[2] When God had regard for Abel's offering but not for Cain's, Cain became angry and his "face fell" (4:5). Cain's external countenance betrayed an intense inner jealousy leading to the first fratricide and a renunciation of the fundamental social obligation that all people, but especially brothers, have for one another. ("Am I my brother's keeper?" 4:9.) For his sin, Cain was sentenced by God to become a "fugitive and a wanderer" (4:12). Cain laments that he was being driven from the "face of the ground" (*lit. translation of* 4:14) and hidden from God's face. He expressed his grief not in the loss of fellowship with God, but in the loss of divine protection. "Behold, you have driven me today away from the ground, and from your face I shall be hidden. I shall be a fugitive and a wanderer on the earth, and whoever finds me will kill me" (4:14). Just as he viewed God functionally when it came to the produce of the ground, he viewed God's presence with the same pragmatic concern. He didn't want God; he simply wanted God's provision and protection.

Protection and provision constitute a broad biblical theme that stretches from the opening chapter of Genesis until the new

---

2   Bruce K. Waltke, *Genesis: A Commentary* (Grand Rapids, MI: Zondervan, 2001), 97.

creation. The story of creation begins with the world in chaos and emptiness and proceeds through God bringing order (days 1–3) and fullness (days 4–6). These twin themes of order and fullness set a trajectory that is detectable through the whole biblical story, such as in God's covenant assurance to Abram that he would be his shield and great reward (Gen. 15:1). In the absence of God, chaos and emptiness encroach—such as in the flood of Noah—but in his presence, there is safety and succor (e.g., Psalm 23). Abel, as a shepherd, exemplified the promised seed of the woman, who would wander from pasture to pasture in immediate dependence upon God's protection and provision. Cain, as a farmer, exemplified the kind of reliance on human achievement that led to Lamech's abusive boast (Gen. 4:23–24), Babel's idolatrous aspirations (Gen. 11:4), and even Lot's incremental affinity for the city that led him from the mountain pastures of the promised land to citizenship in Sodom (Gen. 13:10–11; 14:12; 19:9). Cain's great fear was being dislodged from the security of technological society, believing that God could only provide for and protect him when he was landed and not uprooted from that land. God met Cain's disbelief with a "not so!" and graciously provided a mark of protection (Gen. 4:15), though Cain's departure to the land of "wandering" ("Nod," 4:16) indicates this protection would be more akin to the sword of the civil magistrate rather than the magisterial covering of God's gracious gaze. Cain epitomized fallen man because he loved God's good gifts more than God's gracious gaze.

Jacob

The story of God's face takes a mysterious turn in the life of Jacob. Though Jacob was the second-born son of Isaac and Rebekah,

God sovereignly decreed beforehand that Jacob would receive the double portion of inheritance of God's promises (Gen. 25:19–28). Nevertheless, from his birth to the ford of Jabbok, Jacob relentlessly, resourcefully, and deceptively strove to gain advantages. He stole the birthright from Esau by playing to Esau's impulsive appetites (Gen. 25:29–34), he deceived Isaac in order to steal the firstborn's blessing (Gen. 27:1–40), and he waged a fourteen-year battle of wits with Laban, his father-in-law (Gen. 29–30). Jacob's manipulative self-reliance only sowed hatred in his brother, forcing Jacob to flee Canaan to find a wife (Gen. 27:41), and that same self-reliance compelled him to return to Canaan due to the rancor it created with Laban (Genesis 31).

On the night Jacob left Canaan, God appeared to him at Bethel and swore to be with him wherever he went, to bring him back, and to fulfill for him all the promises God had made to Abraham and Isaac (Gen. 28:10–17). Nevertheless, Jacob responded, "*If* God will be with me . . . then the LORD shall be my God" (Gen. 28:20–21). True to the meaning of his birth name, "he clutches" or "he supplants," Jacob saw life as a zero-sum game, tit-for-tat, life only gives what is grabbed. Despite this, God was with him as promised during Jacob's sojourn with Laban. Across the brook of Jabbok, however, Esau waited. His anger had had fourteen years to ripen. The prospect of Esau's florid face must have weighed heavily on Jacob and slowed his steps as an increasing weight on his back during his journey home. Indeed, Jacob sent ahead three successive tribute parties to appease his brother, followed by his wives and children, leaving Jacob completely alone in the dark. His isolation epitomized his entire life situation except for God's graciousness, which had not dissuaded him from his manipulative ways.

What ensued is one of the most enigmatic and dramatic scenes in all the Bible. The scene begins with ominous minimalism—"And Jacob was left alone" (Gen. 32:24). With equal minimalism the action is described—"And a man wrestled with him until the breaking of the day" (32:24). The straining, sweat, gasping, and dust are described almost nominally, as if the efforts of at least one party are hardly worth elaboration. At the end of this long night—and, at the end of Jacob's long years of self-reliance—the real drama unfolded.

The identity of the stranger was mysterious at first. He was simply "a man" (32:24). In typical biblical fashion, we learn the identity of this character not through the narrator's prosaic description, but through the man's words and actions. At first he seemed bound by Jacob and unable to prevail (32:26), but Jacob's request makes clear that Jacob is the inferior—"I will not let you go unless you bless me." Before responding, the stranger demanded to know Jacob's name, really more a call for Jacob's self-confession than for the stranger's identification. Indeed, Jacob had been a "clutcher" and "supplanter." Perhaps in contemporary colloquial terms he would have been called "slick." Such self-reliance had left him depleted and without an option except to confess his name. To Jacob's confession the stranger, exercising his now-apparent sovereignty over Jacob, responded by renaming Jacob "Israel," "he who strives with God" (32:28). All of Jacob's conniving has not been with Isaac, Esau, or Laban but with God himself.

The glorious irony of this story mustn't escape us. The one who had named Jacob from the beginning, promised him the inheritance of the greatest promise ever made, and had been with Jacob throughout the fourteen years of sojourn is the one who asked his name. Was Jacob without a clue? Or had the exhausting night begun to open his eyes as the sun began to rise? In a single moment Jacob had come to the end of his resourcefulness while also finally finding the source of ultimate and perfect goodness. The stranger was the very one who first had named him "Jacob." Thus, Jacob named the place "Peniel," which means "face of God," explaining "I have seen God face to face, and yet my life has been delivered" (32:30).

Jacob has had the gracious promises of God all of his days, but only now when all of his stratagems, strength, and strainings are exhausted, only in his complete and utter weakness, only when he is hobbled does he find grace. The paradox is expressed beautifully in Charles Wesley's "Come, O Thou Traveler Unknown."

Come, O Thou Traveler unknown,
Whom still I hold but cannot see;
My company before is gone,
And I am left alone with Thee;
With Thee all night I mean to stay,
And wrestle till the break of day. . . .

Yield to me now, for I am weak,
But confident in self-despair;
Speak to my heart, in blessings speak,
Be conquered by my instant prayer;
Speak, or Thou never hence shalt move,
And tell me if Thy name be Love.[3]

3   Charles Wesley, "Come, O Thou Traveler Unknown," *The Sacred Harp* (Huntsville, AL: Sacred Harp Publishing, 1991), 95.

Jacob had petitioned during the wrestling match for two things: (1) the stranger's blessing and (2) the stranger's name. Four hundred years later, Aaron would be instructed to bless the people, Jacob's descendants, with the assurance of God's face shining upon them such that God's name was placed upon them (Num. 6:23–27). Though it would be generations before Aaron receives this command, this episode is pregnant with the Aaronic blessing because Jacob realized that he asked for these blessings from God himself and named the place Peniel, "face of God." Though in a veiled, mysterious way and before the full light of day had dawned, Jacob experienced God's gracious gaze when he came to the end of his own resourcefulness.

Moses

The face of God enters once again into the story of Israel in the life and ministry of Moses. Moses's encounter with the face of God is unparalleled in the Old Testament. We know Moses encountered the glory of God at the burning bush on Sinai when he was called by God to lead Israel out of Egypt (Exodus 3). Later at Mount Sinai once again with the now-redeemed nation in tow, Moses ascended into the cloud and fire while the people remained trembling below (Ex. 20:18–21). As Moses received the Law on the mountain, the people became restless and in spite of God's miraculous plagues, deliverance from Egypt, and presence on the mountain, they demanded that Aaron make them "gods" (plural) who would "go before" them to continue the journey (Ex. 32:1). Both their demand for a pantheon (instead of a single god) as well as the calf form of Aaron's workmanship revealed a tragic equivocation of trust. Accustomed to the pantheons of the surrounding peoples and the several bovine deities of Egypt, the petition of the people and the production of their priest foreshadowed the divided hearts that would leave this first generation out of Egypt short of their promised inheritance in Canaan.

While the demand for gods to "go before us" undoubtedly expressed the desire for a god to lead them on, it's not incidental that Aaron answered this desire with a visible idol. The Hebrew word for "before" is actually the compound of the preposition "to" or "for" with the word for face (*lě* + *pāneh*). While I am not suggesting "before" here literally means "before our faces," their shrouded God and missing mediator Moses caused them to want to walk by sight and not by faith. The inertia of unbelieving minds is always toward visible creation and away from the invisible Creator.

When God learned of the people's sin, he called Moses to step aside in order for God to bring swift judgment upon the people (Ex. 32:10). Instead of stepping aside, Moses interceded on behalf of the people, appealing to God's honor and to God's sworn promise to Abraham centuries earlier (Ex. 32:11–13). God relented from visiting his full wrath upon the people (Ex. 32:14) and affirmed his promise to bring them to the promised land, yet he announced that he himself would not go with them (Ex. 33:1–3), but only provide an angel to lead them. When the word of this spread to the people they were grieved and humbled themselves (Ex. 33:4–6). This is the context in which we are told of the pattern of intimate communication that existed between God and Moses (Ex. 33:7–11).

When Moses would enter the tent, the people would rise, watch, and worship (Ex. 33:8, 10) as the glory cloud also entered the tent. This describes not just a one-time encounter, but a pattern displaying God's visible indication that Moses was God's chosen person through whom God revealed himself to his people. The narrative then turns from simple description to qualitative comment to say, "Thus the LORD used to speak to Moses face to face, as a man speaks to his friend" (Ex. 33:11).

What does face-to-face mean? Commentators are quick to point out that we mustn't take it literally since within the next few verses God will also say, "You cannot see my face, for man shall not see me and live" (Ex. 33:20). Yet in being too quick to exclude a literal sense, we risk failing to perceive the intimacy conveyed by the expression. Moses spoke with God in-person, person-to-person as it were. As we inhabit a world today in which in-person interpersonal interaction is declining and even eschewed, this description calls us back to a longing for the interpersonal intimacy implied and required of our embodied lives. The necessities of life often remove us from the presence of many of those we love most, but we are still creatures with bodies. More particularly, we are creatures with faces, created to know and be known by others in one another's presence.

The narrative's "interruption" of Moses's intercession is not really an interruption. It is a reminder and an amplification for us to see what kind of man was interceding on behalf of the nation of Israel. Though not a man of absolute moral perfection, Moses was of such a consecrated life that he could go up the mountain and into the tent. As we will see, consecration is the prerequisite to beholding God's gracious gaze. This face-to-face-ness is the venue from where Moses interceded. His model intercession appealed to God's glory (i.e., reputation), goodness, and covenant (Ex. 32:11–14). Though

God would have seen to it that the people made it to the promised land without God's presence, that was not enough for Moses, for to have the land without the Lord would be to have nothing (Ex. 33:15). Moses's face-to-face intercession prevailed, and God answered, "My presence (*lit.*, "face") will go with you" (Ex. 33:14). "This very thing that you have spoken I will do, for you have found favor in my sight, and I know you by name" (Ex. 33:17).

Emboldened perhaps by his successful intercession and enticed by the beauty of God's presence, Moses asked further, "Please show me your glory" (Ex. 33:18). God replied, "You cannot see my face, for man shall not see me and live" (Ex. 33:20). However he continued, "While my glory passes by I will put you in a cleft of the rock, and I will cover you with my hand until I have passed by. Then I will take away my hand, and you shall see my back, but my face shall not be seen" (Ex. 33:22–23). This is the most intimate encounter with God of any in the entire Old Testament, setting the stage for the Aaronic blessing which follows this encounter shortly, but more importantly it provides the backdrop for the appearance of the glory of God in Christ.

"My Voice You Heard"

It was Israel's privilege as God's chosen people to hear him speak to the whole nation face-to-face from Mount Sinai (Deut. 5:4). Their possession of the law, along with God's mighty works on their behalf, constituted their distinctive witness among the nations (Deut. 4:6–8). Before reminding them of that privilege, God gave an ominous warning against idolatry (Deut. 4:15–31) and recapitulated the awesome way in which he had appeared and spoken to them.

You heard the sound of words, but saw no form; there was only a voice. (Deut. 4:12)

Did any people ever hear the voice of a god speaking out of the midst of the fire, as you have heard, and still live? (Deut. 4:33)

Israel must remember that God didn't speak to them in the same way as he did with Moses, but at their insistence at Sinai, God spoke to them *through* Moses (Deut. 18:15–17). They must listen to God by listening to Moses if they wish to choose life rather than death (Deut. 30:19). After all, Moses was the prophet *par excellence*, the measuring stick for every subsequent prophet and the paradigm for a greater prophet like him whom God would raise up one day (Deut. 18:15, 18).

Throughout his tenure of leadership, Moses was so closely associated with God's actions and words, that at times Moses is described as the one who did the mighty works (Deut. 34:10–12) and the one in whom the people were to believe (Ex. 14:31). Thus the final scene of Moses's life as he ascended Mount Pisgah to look over into the promised land, which he himself would not enter, ends with the epitaph: "And there has not arisen a prophet since in Israel like Moses, whom the LORD knew face to face . . ." (Deut. 34:10). The one who spoke to God face-to-face is now declared to be *known* by God with the same level of intimacy.

Deuteronomy, which stresses the incomparability of Yahweh, closes with an acknowledgment of the incomparability of Moses himself. Indeed, one Jewish tradition links God and Moses beautifully by imagining God declaring, "Moses said of me, 'There is none like Yahweh,' and so I in turn bear witness that 'There is none like Moses.'"[4] To know God face-to-face was the acme of human existence, and the privilege was uniquely Moses's. This is the context in which Aaron was commissioned to declare the blessing of God's gracious gaze upon God's people.

Conclusion

I recently purchased eyeglasses online. While online shopping accesses a greater variety of options, it has the disadvantage of not providing the same "look and feel" possibilities of a retail store. While the feel is hard to duplicate online, the online eyeglass providers allowed me to upload a personal photograph and superimpose frames on my photograph's face to see what they'd look like on me. This experience mirrors one of the primary functions of biblical narratives. While in one sense the whole Bible is about God, the vast parade of biblical characters provides us with mirrors to hold up next to ourselves. While this is a basic technique for reading all narratives, whether children's fables or Victorian novels, it's an especially important way to read biblical narratives. As you read, I encourage you to think: *Who in this particular story resembles me the most in their words, actions, and attitudes? What would I have done in that situation? Who should I emulate? Whose example convicts me of similar ignorance and error?*

Are we like Adam and Eve in the fresh glow of creation's dawn, seeing our Maker in sinless bliss? Of course not, but do we have a longing in us to see what only they had seen? Are we, like them, hiding from God's face in the garden—Adam with back bowed and face downcast under the futility of thorns and thistles, daily

4   Christopher Wright, *Deuteronomy*, New International Biblical Commentary (Peabody, MA: Hendrickson, 1996), 313.

looking at the dust that will one day reclaim him? Are we like Cain with averted gaze, desiring protection and provision from living in the light of God's face but unwilling to bring ourselves to look into God's face because of our unbending self-reliance? Are we like Jacob, having spent our lives cultivating a religious self-reliance by grasping what God has freely promised us, only to find that God, in his fatherly discipline, has stripped away all of our tricks and efforts in order to bring us low and confront us in the dark night of the soul? Have we wrestled with God in the night so that now we walk with a limp of grace, having seen the face of God? While Moses occupied a unique role that only Jesus Christ ultimately fulfills (Heb. 3:5), are we so enticed with the beatific vision of seeing God's face that seeking God's face is the pearl of great price, the treasure in whose light "the things of earth will grow strangely dim"?[5] Each of these characters are key figures in Israel's origin story and offer themselves to us so that we might long for the look of God's gracious gaze.

For Further Reflection

1. Try to come up with a title or a slogan to describe each person or phase of relating to the face of God. For example, Adam and Eve before the fall might be "unfettered facetime" or Jacob might be "low light exposure." See if you can have fun with different ideas.

2. Are there any persons or phases in encountering the face of God with which you identify most? Or are there periods in your life that seem a lot like these Old Testament episodes?

Helen Howarth Lemmel, "Turn Your Eyes upon Jesus," *Trinity Hymnal*, rev. ed. (Atlanta: Great Commission Publications, 1997), no. 481.

3. What have you learned about yourself as you have read about the persons and phases of the prequel to God's gracious gaze?

4. Having reflected on the people and stages of the revelation of God's face, take time to pray Psalm 27's aspiration, "My heart says to you, 'Your face, Lord, do I seek'" (v. 8).

2

The Meaning of
Numbers 6:22–27

The Content of the Blessing

MY FAMILY MOVED TO CENTRAL FLORIDA at the height of the space shuttle program. As we were getting acclimated and spending time with local families, among the things we were told to anticipate were the rocket launches from Cape Canaveral. Even though we lived nearly fifty miles away, we were assured that they were spectacular sights. Skeptically, we asked our friends how to know exactly where to look. They assured us that if we simply looked east, we would have no trouble seeing the event. Our friends were right. In September of that year STS-48, Discovery, launched in the early evening. As advised, we watched the countdown on television until the moment of liftoff, and then we rushed out into the backyard to see if we could spot it. Though it was still just a few more minutes to sunset, the rocket lit up the entire eastern sky and even illuminated our backyard dozens of miles away. As I turned to look at the rest of the family, I could even see the light reflected on their faces. The light was so powerful and bright that it left no question about where to look.

As we have begun to see from chapter 1, seeing the face of God was the chief delight of the blissful creation, the most grievous loss after the fall, and the tantalizing prospect of the covenant community. The "blessed hope" of Christ's future return (Titus 2:13) and the "beatific vision" or *visio Dei* ("vision of God") of seeing God face-to-face (1 Cor. 13:12) await believers in the future and are the basis of the Christian hope. Everyone will know where to look at Christ's return, for "every eye will see him" (Rev. 1:7). When we see God in our glorified state, whether bodily or spiritually, the light of God will have displaced the sun and moon (Rev. 21:23).[1] Both on the way to glory and when we are there, God will be the all-consuming vision of his people. But where are we to look in the meantime? Is there a glimpse of the face of God in this life, or was it reserved for only a select few like Moses, Isaiah, and Paul? The Aaronic blessing tells us yes, the face of God shines on his people now, seen not through their eyes but through their ears, through words of benediction.

Having surveyed the prequel context to the blessing of God's gracious gaze, we are now prepared to turn to what the Aaronic blessing says:

---

1 For a discussion of the nature of the beatific vision, see Herman Bavinck, *Reformed Dogmatics: Volume 2, God and Creation*, trans. John Vriend, ed. John Bolt (Grand Rapids, MI: BakerAcademic, 2004), 182–91.

The LORD spoke to Moses, saying, "Speak to Aaron and his sons, saying, Thus you shall bless the people of Israel: you shall say to them,

> The LORD bless you and keep you;
> the LORD make his face to shine upon you and be gracious to you;
> the LORD lift up his countenance upon you and give you peace.

"So shall they put my name upon the people of Israel, and I will bless them." (Num. 6:22–27)

Surrounding Context

Initially in the darkness, Jacob was unsure whether the stranger at the Jabbok was friend or foe. As Joshua reconnoitered Jericho, he was unsure whether the man standing before him was "for us, or for our adversaries" (Josh. 5:13). Both dramatic scenes were resolved with God's response, being more or less, "I am God." He blessed hobbled Jacob. He gave victory to prostrate Joshua. To comprehend the "breadth and length and height and depth" of God's gracious gaze administered through Aaron, we needed to recognize the drama in its larger context. Having surveyed the history of God's gracious gaze in chapter 1, we must now consider the blessing's immediate context within the book of Numbers.

The surrounding context of God's gracious gaze is fundamentally twofold—redemption and consecration. Israel, in fulfillment of the promise God made to Abraham, was redeemed from slavery in Egypt by a succession of God's mighty acts so that they stood at the foot of Mount Sinai a redeemed people, a people saved by God's grace (Deuteronomy 4). It is vitally important to understand that the law was given as a gift to an already-redeemed people rather than as a condition for their salvation. Israel did not trade God's grace for the law when they responded, "All that the LORD has spoken we will do" (Ex. 19:8). Given their status as a redeemed people, Israel's identity and purpose was declared by God.

> You yourselves have seen what I did to the Egyptians, and how I bore you on eagles' wings and brought you to myself. Now therefore, if you will indeed obey my voice and keep my covenant, you shall be my treasured possession among all peoples, for all the earth is mine; and you shall be to me a kingdom of priests and a holy nation. (Ex. 19:4–6)

Though still a people able to sin, and who sinned famously at times, this presented a dilemma. How could a sinful people be a priestly people mediating God's blessings to the nations? What's more, this royal priestly calling involved the very dwelling of God among them. As God said to Aaron the high priest,

> I will dwell among the people of Israel and will be their God. And they shall know that I am the LORD their God, who brought them out of the land of Egypt that I might dwell among them. I am the LORD their God. (Ex. 29:45–46; reiterated in Lev. 26:12–13)

The immanent presence of God required that God's people be holy like God (Lev. 11:44). This highlights a crucial aspect of the law of God often overlooked. The law of God was given to a people under grace with commands and prohibitions about right and holy living, but it also included provisions for when the people were unrighteous and unholy. This is apparent in the instructions for the tabernacle that immediately followed the laws of Exodus. "And let them make me a sanctuary, that I may dwell in their midst" (Ex. 25:8). "Sanctuary" derives from the word for "holiness." The holy God's holy dwelling would be among the people. But at the very center of that holy dwelling was the *kappōret*, the "atonement covering" (usually translated as "mercy seat"), the lid on top of the ark (Ex. 25:17). The tablets of stone were kept inside the ark. It was there that God, through Moses and Aaron, would speak to his people. "There I will meet with you, and from above the mercy seat, from between the two cherubim that are on the ark of the testimony, I will speak with you about all that I will give you in commandment for the people of Israel" (Ex. 25:22). This is the same place where the blood on the Day of Atonement was sprinkled (Lev. 16:14–15). While the law dictated the moral terms on which the holy God would dwell among a people capable of sinning, the law also provided the remedies for when sin threatened that relationship. This concept is demonstrated on a larger scale with the book of Leviticus in which the so-called "Holiness Code" (Lev. 17–26) governed diet, hygiene, relationships with surrounding peoples, and the days and seasons of the year. Nothing was exempt from God's holy claims. The cleansing grace that God's people needed to behold God's holy face shining upon them was provided for in the very law that demanded holiness as they practiced the law by faith in their gracious God.

Immediate Context

The more immediate context of the Aaronic blessing is the book of Numbers. Numbers recounts the journey of Israel from Mount Sinai to the promised land.[2] Numbers begins and ends with censuses of men of fighting age of the first and second generations, respectively. Since counting troops was a prerequisite to war, Numbers anticipates the holy war that Israel will wage as they enter the land. The first generation saved out of Egypt had not trusted the Lord, had constantly tested him, and were often tempted to turn back to Egypt. Thus, that first generation would perish in the wilderness short of the promised land. Written at the end of their forty years of wandering, Numbers was a witness of God's faithfulness to the second generation in spite of the first generation's failure. It summoned the second generation to fully trust in God and Joshua in the conquest. If God was in their midst, they would possess the land, but for God to be in their midst they must consecrate themselves to him.

Therefore, after the census and the arrangement of the camp into a marching formation (Numbers 1–2), the duties of the Levitical priests are spelled out according to their clans and a series of final matters are addressed regarding the consecration of the people (Numbers 3–6). These final matters included removing uncleanness from the camp (Num. 5:1–4), restitution for interpersonal sins (5:5–10), adultery (5:11–31), and the stipulations pertaining to Nazarites, a particular order of holy men who weren't priests (6:1–21). All these matters in Numbers 1:1–6:21 have

2   For a more comprehensive look at Numbers, see Michael J. Glodo, "Numbers," *Biblical-Theological Introduction to the Old Testament*, ed. Miles Van Pelt (Wheaton, IL: Crossway, 2016), 107–31.

something in common. They involve the deeply serious subject of consecration, of setting the people apart.

The need for consecration points back to the whole sequence of events when Israel was freed from slavery in Egypt, commissioned as a royal priesthood at Mount Sinai, and given God's law through Moses. The purpose of this sequence is encapsulated in God's promise "And I will walk among you and will be your God, and you shall be my people" (Lev. 26:12; cf. Ex. 6:7; 29:45–46). God's intent to dwell among his people is at the heart of God's promises to his people. It was the *sine qua non* of Moses's intercession following the golden calf. It would later be the aspiration of Solomon's prayer to see God's glory dwell in the temple (1 Kings 8:11). At creation, God had walked among his royal priests (Adam and Eve) in the Edenic sanctuary. But currently, on the plains of Moab, it was in the tabernacle and through the priests that God dwelt among his people. As a priestly nation, they must be consecrated so that God would be with them, not against them as in the times of great national sin and divine punishment (Exodus 32; Numbers 21; Joshua 7). Even though God's moral perfection necessitated holiness on the part of his people if he was to dwell among them, God graciously provided the means for repentance and restoration. Yet repentance and restoration only reset the relationship. Consecration, the people giving themselves wholly over to the Lord, was necessary for their holy calling to be God's people. The gift of God's gracious gaze in the Aaronic blessing is not given with God's eyes shut toward sin or a compromise of his own holiness or at some moment of transient moral perfection by his people. Rather it is an ongoing gift enjoyed through a whole ritual system that required and provided the means for consecration. Similar to God's glory filling the tabernacle in Exodus 40, signifying that it had been built and its priest consecrated according to the divine requirements revealed to Moses on Mount Sinai (Ex. 25:1–9), so the Aaronic blessing is the divine response to Israel's consecration according to God's gracious provisions.

With the larger background of the prequel of God's face, the surrounding context of being a redeemed people, and the immediate context of consecration in view, we can now begin to reflect upon the words of the Aaronic blessing itself.

The Blessing Itself

According to art historians, when picture frames began to appear in the eleventh century, they were often created as part of the artwork itself. Indeed, frames often are an important part of presenting visual art in museums and galleries even today. This artistic framing can be true of literary works such as the Aaronic blessing as well. A literary frame not only provides context to the blessing Aaron was to speak, but the frame itself is part of this literary work of art. Aaron's blessing is framed by a narrative of divine speech at the beginning and the end, which contributes significantly to its meaning.

The LORD spoke to Moses, saying, "Speak to Aaron and his sons, saying, Thus you shall bless the people of Israel: you shall say to them . . . (Num. 6:22)

So shall they put my name upon the people of Israel, and I will bless them. (6:27)

Table 2.1: The Stairway of the Blessing

Narrative Frame
"So shall they put my name upon the people of Israel, and I will bless them."

Line 3
the LORD lift up his countenance upon you and give you peace.

Line 2
the LORD make his face to shine upon you and be gracious to you;

Line 1
The LORD bless you and keep you;

Narrative Frame
The LORD spoke to Moses, saying, "Speak to Aaron and his sons, saying, Thus you shall bless the people of Israel: you shall say to them,

The first portion of the frame makes it clear that in Aaron's word God was acting. Aaron spoke for God. The closing frame reveals the effect of the blessing, the placing of God's name upon Israel. God's intent from beginning to end is to bless his people by placing his name upon them.

If we were to read the blessing itself in Hebrew, we would immediately notice several things about the form of the blessing. It consists of three lines of three, five, and seven words and fifteen, twenty, and twenty-five consonants, respectively. With the narrative frame's announced intent of blessing, the concluding frame's climax of placing the divine name on the people, and the proportion and progression in length of the three lines of the blessing, we can observe stair steps, like the steps that might lead up into a temple (see Table 2.1).

The progression suggested by the form is confirmed in the substance of bless/keep, face/gracious, and lift up/peace. Each line involves a divine action with a consequence of that action. The divine action, expressed in the narrative frame's intent to "bless," (6:24) moves from the generic "bless" in the first line, to the hospitable "shine" (6:25), culminating in the life-giving "lift up" (6:26). Moreover, the divine action in each line is the cause for the respective results.

Table 2.2: Divine Word and Result

Cause		Effect
bless	→	keep/guard
shine	→	grace
countenance	→	peace

God's blessing will "keep" (6:24), a word often meaning "guard" in cultic contexts. The shining of God's face bestows divine favor or grace (6:25). The lifting up of God's countenance, the same Hebrew word for "face" as in the previous line, brings "peace" or *shalom*, the highest state of human flourishing (6:26). The lines of the blessing are like the waves of the sea breaking farther and farther during a rising tide, raising the people's faces progressively upward.

Verbs in all languages have "moods." For example, the *imperative mood* is how we express commands. "Come here!" is an imperative. The verbs of the Aaronic blessing are in the *jussive mood*, not quite the imperative but expressing a strong wish or desire. In English we often express this by adding the words "let" or "may." Similarly when one person says to another "Have a nice day!" it isn't technically an imperative—we can't order someone to have a good day—but a wish that the person might have a nice day, and perhaps a reminder for the person to expect and do their part to have a nice day!

Though the initial verbs in each line are in the jussive mood, they are more than a wish or desire because of the one who is speaking. As Aaron spoke these words of blessing, he did so according to God's command and authorization. It is abundantly clear that it is the Lord, not Aaron, who is the source of this blessing. Aaron spoke for God himself. Therefore, Aaron's words are God's way of taking action. If we step back to take in the whole biblical picture, we realize quickly that God's words are not ever mere words. God's words are his actions. God does things by speaking. In the beginning "God said" and "it was" (Genesis 1). When God in Christ called Lazarus to come forth from the tomb, it was the voice of Christ that raised Lazarus from the dead. It is because God acts with his word that Isaiah the prophet could say, "So shall my word be that goes out from my mouth; it shall not return to me empty, but it shall accomplish that which I purpose, and shall succeed in the thing for which I sent it" (Isa. 55:11).

When a child challenges a parent's instructions with "Why?" an impatient parent may reply, "Because I said so." That response may or may not elicit the desired obedience. But when it is God who speaks, his word defines reality. As God speaks through his priest to his redeemed and consecrated people, the Aaronic blessing is more than just God's well wishes for his people. God's spoken word assures his people that it will be so.

God's Word Is God's Deed

If God's word equals action, how did God's blessing determine Israel's reality? God's word of blessing circumscribed the world, meaning the world is the way God said. He is the sovereign God who created and rules over all things according to his wise design and his wise ways. The way the world is and the way the world goes is under his command. Even as Israel passed through the "howling waste of the wilderness" (Deut. 32:10), the cloud and fire of God's glory overshadowed them. In the chaotic world at the end of the first century when followers of Christ were experiencing hostility because of their faith, God (through the apostle John) parted the curtains of heaven with the vision of Revelation 4 to reassure his people that he was on the throne and the world was under his command. The saints of the Old Testament sang, "He who keeps Israel will neither slumber nor sleep . . . he will keep your life" (Ps. 121:4, 7). Why? Because their "help comes from the LORD who made heaven and earth" (121:2). Their Redeemer was also the sovereign Creator (Isa. 43:1).

Bless and Keep

Each of the blessings, the three "steps" toward God's presence, have a particular meaning. The first, "The LORD bless you and keep you" (Num. 6:24), assures the people of God's protection and preservation. "Keep" in this context includes the sense of guarding and protecting. This keeping draws on the larger biblical motif of shield and reward promised to Abraham (Gen. 15:1). God had protected Israel from exposure to the harsh elements of the wilderness and threats posed by the various peoples they encountered on the way to the promised land. The Aaronic blessing both reminded Israel of God's protection and enacted that protection as God's word-deed.

"Keeping" means not only protection *from* but preserving *for*. At times the greatest threat to Israel was Israel itself, or rather God when Israel violated God's holiness. Principal among the duties of the Levites was to "keep" (i.e., "guard") the tabernacle spaces against unauthorized intrusion (Num. 1:53; 3:7–8). Soon Israel would learn that faithful servants like Phinehas were necessary to maintain the holiness of the community lest God himself "break out" against Israel (Ex. 19:22, 24). Aaron's son Phineas proved to be a faithful priestly instrument of God's keeping when he not only guarded the camp from the corruptions of Baal worship but preserved the people from the consuming wrath of God (Numbers 25, esp. v. 11). Consequently, God honored Phinehas with a "covenant of peace" (25:12) because his zeal preserved the *shalom* (peace) of God's presence among his people.

Even today under the new covenant, church leaders should foster the blessing of God's people by guarding them and protecting them from external as well as internal danger. Paul exhorted the elders from Ephesus to pay attention to the flock because "fierce wolves will come in among you" (Acts 20:28–29). It is the responsibility of God's people to readily embrace their spiritual guardians so that the leaders who "are keeping watch over [our] souls" can do so with joy (Heb. 13:17). Our leaders do so as instruments of the good shepherd's promise that no one would snatch us from his hand (John 10:28).

God protects and preserves his people because they are his "treasured possession" (Ex. 19:5; 1 Pet. 2:9). Our contemporary sensibilities may make us pause at the notion of being God's "possession." After all, a "possessive" relationship implies a controlling dynamic or mentality. Jesus warned his disciples about the Gentile rulers who "lord it over" their people (Mark 10:42). Yet if we have reservations about being God's possession, it is more likely due either to experience of abusive human relationships or a belief in Western individualism. God's people are twice God's, having been *created* and *redeemed* by him, and he will keep us.

> But now thus says the LORD,
> he who created you, O Jacob,
>   he who formed you, O Israel:
> "Fear not, for I have redeemed you;
>   I have called you by name, you are mine.
> When you pass through the waters, I will be with you;
>   and through the rivers, they shall not overwhelm you;
> when you walk through fire you shall not be burned,
>   and the flame shall not consume you." (Isa. 43:1–2)

God's people are his "treasured possession" (Ex. 19:5; Deut. 7:6; 14:2). We are the apple of his eye (Deut. 32:10), whom he jealously guards (Zech. 2:8). We are our Beloved's and he is ours (Song 6:3; 7:10). The Lord blesses his people by keeping them (Num. 6:24).

Shining Face and Grace

The second line of the blessing says the Lord will also be gracious to his people by making his face to shine upon them (Num. 6:25). We may imagine a person brought before a king in a royal court, perhaps seeking justice in a legal case or a gracious favor in exchange for some act of loyalty. The person's life, or at least well-being, is in the king's hands, and the supplicant searches the king's face for some nonverbal indication of the king's disposition. *What kind of mood is he in? Is he attentive to the cause? What does his face say about his intentions?* In this ancient world, kings' countenances were at times depicted in art with halos or coronas around their heads to indicate the king's special status with the gods. Proverbs uses this imagery to describe the blessing of a wise king:

> A king's wrath is a messenger of death,
> and a wise man will appease it.
> In the light of a king's face there is life,
> and his favor is like the clouds that bring the spring rain.
> (Prov. 16:14–15)

Thus, when God assures his people that his face will shine on them, he is declaring his favorable disposition toward them. The shining face of God throughout the Old Testament and particularly in the Psalms is the beatific vision.

We may at some point stop to ponder the nature of the meta-phor of God's face. After all, God is a spirit and, as God, does not have a body (Rom. 1:20; 1 John 4:12). The expression is a metaphor. However, we would be misinformed to think of it as a "mere metaphor." Biblical metaphors are rarely mere figures of speech, but often powerful means of projecting reality. God is a rock, father, shepherd, king, and a tower, just to name a few.

Many metaphors in everyday life determine consciously or sub-consciously how we understand and act in the world.[3] Biblical metaphors are intended to have an even greater power to shape our outlook and actions. They are not simply fancy figures of speech that the inspired writers of Scripture used to decorate their meaning. Biblical metaphors shape our reality. "The heavens declare the glory of God, and the sky above proclaims his handiwork" (Ps. 19:1). God's invisible attributes are revealed in creation (Rom. 1:20). God designed the world in order to reveal himself through it as the "theater of his glory."[4] So the hymn declares, "God, all nature sings thy glory,"[5] because God created the world for the purpose of revealing himself through that created order. Walking by faith rather than by sight is to live by the metaphors of Scripture (such as the kingdom of God; Christ the good shepherd; the church as a body, bride, mother, commonwealth, city, etc.), even though we don't see these things literally with our eyes. They are, the Bible tells us,

3   For more on the reality-shaping effect of metaphors, see George Lakoff and Mark Johnson, *Metaphors We Live By* (Chicago: University of Chicago Press, 1980).

4   John Calvin, *Institutes of the Christian Religion*, 2 vols., ed. John T. McNeil, trans. Ford Lewis Battles, The Library of Christian Classics (Philadelphia, PA: Westminter Press, 1960), I.v.8 (1:61); I.vi.2 (1:72); I.xiv.20 (1:179); II.vi.1 (1:341).

5   David Clowney, "God, All Nature Sings Thy Glory," *Trinity Hymnal*, rev. ed. (Atlanta: Great Commission Publications, 1997), no. 122.

even more real than what our eyes can see. "For we walk by faith, not by sight" (2 Cor. 5:7). The face of God in the beatific vision is arguably the most transcendent metaphor in all of Scripture.

God's Face in the Psalms

The Aaronic blessing provides the well from which the Psalms draw and reflect the implications of God's gracious gaze. Like the olive trees of Zechariah's vision that supplied an endless reserve of oil to light the golden lampstand (Zech. 4:1–7), the Aaronic blessing is the source of the light of God's face in the spirituality of Israel found in Psalms. For example, the light of God's face is the source of benevolence and joy:

> There are many who say, "Who will show us some good?
>   Lift up the light of your face upon us, O Lord!"
> You have put more joy in my heart
>   than they have when their grain and wine abound.
>   (Ps. 4:6–7)

As such, God's face is the basis for the psalmist's plea for vindication and for exhorting others to put their confidence in God (4:1, 3, 5). His confidence in the Lord allows him to lie down and sleep "in peace" (4:8). Those who put their trust in the Lord will reflect God's radiance:

> I sought the Lord, and he answered me
>   and delivered me from all my fears.
> Those who look to him are radiant,
>   and their faces shall never be ashamed. (Ps. 34:4–5)

Even in the midst of great suffering, God's countenance is the psalmist's hope:

> For he has not despised or abhorred
>> the affliction of the afflicted,
> and he has not hidden his face from him,
>> but has heard, when he cried to him. (Ps. 22:24)

> Make your face shine on your servant;
>> save me in your steadfast love!
> O Lord, let me not be put to shame,
>> for I call upon you;
> let the wicked be put to shame;
>> let them go silently to Sheol. (Ps. 31:16–17)

The psalmist recalls Israel's victory in possessing the promised land as a victory of the Lord's doing. God's mighty arm, a frequent metaphor to describe the power of God doing mighty acts to save his people, is paralleled by reference to God's beaming countenance:

> For not by their own sword did they win the land,
>> nor did their own arm save them,
> but your right hand and your arm,
>> and the light of your face, for you delighted in them. (Ps. 44:3)

God's face is thought to be hidden when enemies seem to be getting the upper hand:

Awake! Why are you sleeping, O Lord?
    Rouse yourself! Do not reject us forever!
Why do you hide your face?
    Why do you forget our affliction and oppression?
        (Ps. 44:23–24)

The thought that God would hide his face from his people is a cause for despair:

How long, O LORD? Will you forget me forever?
    How long will you hide your face from me?
How long must I take counsel in my soul
    and have sorrow in my heart all the day?
How long shall my enemy be exalted over me? (Ps. 13:1–2;
      see also 69:16; 88:14)

Psalm 67 generously draws upon the Aaronic blessing to underscore Israel's priestly mission. Its beginning plea is an overt echo of the blessing tied directly to its purpose indicated by "that":

May God be gracious to us and bless us
    and make his face to shine upon us, *Selah*
that your way may be known on earth,
    your saving power among all nations.
Let the peoples praise you, O God;
    let all the peoples praise you! (67:1–3)

Thus Psalm 67 ends with confidence that God would do as he promised in the blessing and achieve his ultimate purpose in doing so. "God shall bless us; let all the ends of the earth fear him!" (67:7).

Psalm 80 is a plea for salvation from enemies whose oppressions are God's chastisement for unspecified national sin. The basis for the appeal is God's past acts for and presence among his people. The nation, once a tender vine God plucked out of Egypt and gently planted and nurtured, is now being ravaged by wild beasts (80:8–13). The psalmist appeals to God to restore his presence to his people and make his face to shine on them once again (80:3, 7) so that he might "restore" and save his people (80:19):

> Restore us, O God;
> let your face shine, that we may be saved! (80:3)

Instruction in the law is a means by which God's face shines on his people. "Make your face shine upon your servant, and teach me your statutes" (Ps. 119:135). By taking God's word to heart, his people will be preserved from oppressors (119:134), but neglect of the law is cause for great grief. "My eyes shed streams of tears, because people do not keep your law" (119:136).

John Calvin notably called the Psalms "'an Anatomy of all Parts of the Soul'; for there is not an emotion of which anyone can be conscious that is not here represented as in a mirror."[6] Clearly one of the panels of this mirror of the soul is the Aaronic blessing incorporated into Israel's worship. The role of God's shining face is woven almost inextricably into Israel's piety, including key terms incorporated into the "Psalms of Ascent" (Psalms 120–130).

---

6   John Calvin, *Commentary on the Psalms*, trans. James Anderson, Calvin's Commentaries, vol. 4 (Grand Rapids, MI: Baker, 1984), xxxvii.

God's Hidden Face

While God's favor is expressed as his face turning toward or shining upon his people, conversely, the withdrawal or hiding of God's gracious gaze is identified with God's judgment or perceived abandonment. God threatened in Deuteronomy (the book of God's covenant with the nation) that persistent, hardhearted sin and rebellion would deprive them of the light of his countenance.

> Then my anger will be kindled against them in that day, and I will forsake them and hide my face from them, and they will be devoured. And many evils and troubles will come upon them, so that they will say in that day, "Have not these evils come upon us because our God is not among us?" And I will surely hide my face in that day because of all the evil that they have done, because they have turned to other gods. (Deut. 31:17–18)

Additionally, in desperation Job called out, "Why do you hide your face and count me as your enemy?" (Job 13:24). Echoing the same sentiment is the psalmist when he says, "How long, O LORD? Will you forget me forever? How long will you hide your face from me?" (Ps. 13:1) and,

> Hide not your face from me.
> Turn not your servant away in anger,
>   O you who have been my help.
> Cast me not off; forsake me not,
>   O God of my salvation! (Ps. 27:9)

THE MEANING OF NUMBERS 6:22–27

God's gaze is not gracious toward the unrepentant unrighteous but instead makes for judgment rather than peace (Ps. 34:16). God will even hide his face from his people in severe discipline for their sin:

> There is no one who calls upon your name,
> who rouses himself to take hold of you;
> for you have hidden your face from us,
> and have made us melt in the hand of our iniquities.
> (Isa. 64:7)

For this reason a plea for mercy may be expressed by asking God to turn his face away from personal sin (Ps. 51:9). Only the upright can be confident in seeing God's face (Ps. 11:7; 17:15).

The frequent and rich usage of the imagery of God's face testifies both to the enormity of the concept and how the Aaronic blessing permeates the spiritual life of God's people. For God's people the Aaronic blessing "has continual, permanent, lasting character and meaning. This is the prayer for God's providential care of the community, which is always one and the same, and always responsive to the human situation."[7]

Shalom

The third and climactic element of the Aaronic blessing "peace" (Heb., *šalôm*) is the most comprehensive, incorporating and transcending the other lines that precede it (Num. 6:26). "Peace," in Hebrew *shalom*, is a biblical term that can encompass everyday

---

7   Patrick D. Miller Jr., "The Blessing of God: An Interpretation of Numbers 6:22–27," *Interpretation* 29, no. 3 (July 1975), 248.

uses such as the absence or cessation of hostilities and interpersonal strife. "Peace" can also mean simply inner peace or serenity. These dimensions—the external, the interpersonal, and the internal—are included in God's promise of peace, but shalom in the Aaronic blessing involves much, much more.

Underlying shalom is the idea of wholeness. Its verbal root, for example, is used in biblical laws of restitution, which require the responsible party to make whole the damaged party (Ex. 21:34). The peace offerings signified restored fellowship with God through the act of a priest (representing God) and the offeror eating the offering together. The relationship between the worshiper and God was made whole again. It was the relationship between God and his people to which the shalom of the Aaronic blessing referred, because shalom is covenantal. In a special way, God's gift of shalom to his people was a blessing bestowed as an expression of his covenant commitment to them.

The covenantal character of shalom is reflected in several ways, several of which are brought out in Psalm 85. First, shalom is the fruit of salvation. God will speak "peace" to his people (85:8) because his "salvation is near to those who fear him" (85:9). Remember, Aaron's blessing was administered to the redeemed multitude in the wilderness who had witnessed God's mighty acts delivering them from bondage in Egypt. God's salvation also brings righteousness. It set things right and imposes just conditions such that shalom is a manifestation of God's righteousness (Isa. 32:1–2). "Righteousness and peace kiss each other" (Ps. 85:10). God's redeemed people, therefore, must consecrate themselves to him to be holy as he is holy (Lev. 11:44) and live lives wholly devoted to him. In other words, they are to "fear him" (Ps. 85:9).

Steadfast love and faithfulness meet;
  righteousness and peace kiss each other.
Faithfulness springs up from the ground,
  and righteousness looks down from the sky.
    (Ps. 85:10–11)

God's Presence

The covenantal character of shalom in which God's faithfulness to his people is reflected in salvation, consecration, and righteousness is an outgrowth of shalom's most profound dimension—the presence of God. Shalom exists when God is present among his people, because all expressions of shalom are the consequences of God's presence. People were created to have fellowship with God, and though that fellowship was disrupted by the fall, at the heart of God's covenant commitment to Israel was his promise that he would be their God, they would be his people, and he would dwell in their midst (Ex. 6:7; 29:45; Lev. 26:12).

This presence is more than God's omnipresence. Yes, God is always present everywhere, but he manifests his special presence among his people in order to be known by and rule directly among them. This presence is most observable in *theophanies*, instances in which God dramatically and visibly manifests his presence. This was his manner with Adam and Eve in Eden before the fall, Abraham in the smoking firepot, Jacob at Bethel and Penuel, Moses at the burning bush, and all Israel on Mount Sinai. In fact, that glorious theophanic presence—the "glory of God"—was with Israel from the shores of the Red Sea until their entry into the promised land, shading them by day, warming them by night, and marching before them through the barren wilderness. God's immanent presence brought provisions as well as promises, provisions of bread and water in the wilderness and milk and honey in the promised land. God's *shalom* wasn't a mere word, but the result of a visible, material state of affairs—a state of bliss—resulting from God's presence.

We often speak of the promised land as "the Holy Land," but the land was holy only because of God's presence. God didn't simply create a paradise and toss Israel the keys to live there. The vitality of the land was because of God's active presence. It enjoyed protection and abundant provision because of God's active involvement. The land was God's agent to administer blessings for the people's obedience and to withhold blessings for disobedience (Deuteronomy 28). God was not an absentee landlord. Thus shalom is the world where God and his people dwell together in the bliss of divine-human communion:

> Righteousness and justice are the foundation of your throne;
>> steadfast love and faithfulness go before you.
> Blessed are the people who know the festal shout,
>> who walk, O LORD, in the light of your face. . . .
>> (Ps. 89:14–15)

The Name of the Lord

The cumulative effect of the threefold blessing is found in the concluding frame, "So shall they put my name upon the people of Israel, and I will bless them" (Num. 6:27). Aaron and his descendants after him would place the name of Yahweh upon the people to bless them with the fullness that God's presence afforded (Ps. 16:11). To bear the name of God meant possessing his fullness, for his name expresses his attributes:

> The LORD descended in the cloud and stood with him there, and proclaimed the *name* of the LORD. The LORD passed before him and proclaimed, "The LORD, the LORD, a God merciful and gracious, slow to anger, and abounding in steadfast love and faithfulness, keeping steadfast love for thousands, forgiving iniquity and transgression and sin, but who will by no means clear the guilty, visiting the iniquity of the fathers on the children and the children's children, to the third and the fourth generation." (Ex. 34:5–7)

It was God's name upon which Seth called in the world after exile from Eden and upon which Abram called when he arrived in the land of promise (Gen. 4:26; 12:8). God's name was the name revealed to Moses before the burning bush (Ex. 6:2–3) as God prepared his people to witness his mighty acts on their behalf. At times God's name was regarded almost as God himself (Ex. 23:20–21). God's "presence" or "face" was synonymous to God's power, the means by which God had saved his people. The psalmist saw that God saved his people by means of his presence (Ps. 54:1). How was God present? He was present in the form of his "name."

God had promised one day to choose a place for his name to dwell, the one and only place where Israel was to worship him (Deut. 12:11, 21; 14:23–24; 16:2, 6, 11; 26:2). Before that time, in the wilderness, God's presence had filled the tabernacle after it had been made according to the instructions God gave Moses on Mount Sinai (Ex. 25:8–9; 40:34–38). Now, in the Aaronic blessing, God would place his name on his people, which would distinguish them from all other peoples on earth while conferring upon them the stewardship of that name. The Aaronic blessing administered regularly would be both action and reminder, both the act of bestowing his name with all the attendant benefits and a reminder of the great responsibility of bearing his name.

"Yahweh" (often translated as "LORD" in our English translations), the special name by which God was known to his people, is found in the opening frame and in each of the three lines of blessing. It also occurs in the closing frame as the climax to the blessing. Though God would one day choose a special place where his name would dwell (Deut. 12:5), here in the wilderness through his servant Aaron, God placed his name on his people. It was the name of the Lord that Moses and all Israel were to proclaim (Deut. 32:3), and it was Israel's mission to make God's name famous among the nations through his special relationship with his people (2 Sam. 7:23; Pss. 18:49; 45:17; 72:17). This very name was placed upon his people.

A Better Priesthood

The Aaronic blessing expresses and integrates several important biblical themes: for example, God's name, presence, grace, and peace. Not only do these themes reverberate through Scripture, in a number of passages the biblical writers directly interpret and apply the Aaronic blessing. We can see this direct interpretation in Psalms 4, 27, and 67 (as described previously). In an ironic turn, however, through the prophet Malachi, God himself expounds the blessing in an oracle of woe to the priests of postexilic Israel.

The light of God's face distinguished Israel from every other nation. The hard lessons of exile were intended to keep Israel from taking God's presence for granted in the future. Sadly, the last of the minor prophets, Malachi, indicates this presumption had not been cured. Malachi 1:6–2:9 is a polemic against the very priests to whom the Aaronic blessing had been entrusted. Postexilic Israel, who should have learned the hard lessons of exile—of the severe consequences of idolatry and injustice and presumption about their favored status with God—languished nearly a century after their return to the land through the time of Malachi's ministry. Tokens of promise such as the returnees from exile and the rebuilding of the temple showed that God was at work, but the eschatological vision of restoration was not achieved. As the final chapter of Nehemiah so deflatingly describes, the very kinds of problems that led to exile had not been plucked out by the exile and were beginning to grow again from the roots (Nehemiah 13). As God's people awaited full realization of the restoration promises, their faith was flagging, and they returned to the patterns of the past. God sent his prophet Malachi to confront these patterns in a series of six disputations before offering a warning and a promise of the coming "day of the LORD" (Mal. 4:5). The first of these disputations is aimed specifically at the priests and framed in terms of the Aaronic blessing.

According to Michael Fishbane, "All the key terms of the Priestly Blessing are alluded to, or played upon, in the prophet's diatribe . . . The prophet has taken the contents of the Priestly Blessing—delivered by the priests and with its emphasis on blessing, the sanctity of the divine Name, and such benefactions as protection, favourable countenance, and peace—and *inverted them.*"[8] The polemic begins with the charge that the priests have despised God's "name" (Mal. 1:6). They complain that God has not shown favor toward their defective offerings (1:9) using the same verb as "lift up" in the Aaronic blessing (Num. 6:26). They want God's grace (Mal. 1:9), again a term found in the Aaronic blessing (Num. 6:25). In spite of the vain efforts of these priests, which God rejects, God vows:

> For from the rising of the sun to its setting my name will be great among the nations, and in every place incense will be offered to my name, and a pure offering. For my name will be great among the nations, says the LORD of hosts. (Mal. 1:11)

The fame of God's name was God's purpose in setting his name upon Israel, and that purpose will not be thwarted by a corrupt priesthood. On the coming day of the Lord, God will refine and reconstitute his people so that their priestly mission will be fulfilled:

> Cursed be the cheat who has a male in his flock, and vows it, and yet sacrifices to the Lord what is blemished. For I am a great King, says the LORD of hosts, and my name will be feared among the nations. (Mal. 1:14)

The fate of these priests will be curses instead of blessings, for their ministrations were contrary to the "covenant of fear" that God had made with the priestly tribe of Levi, the priests who stood in awe of God's name (Mal. 2:5) and "walked with [God] in

8 Michael Fishbane, *Biblical Interpretation in Ancient Israel* (Oxford: Oxford University Press, 1985), 332–33, emphasis his.

peace" (2:6). Consequently, these priests will be cursed and their faces covered in dung rather than illuminated by God's face (2:3). God's presence was Israel's greatest possession, yet the glory of the Lord had departed from them due to their stiff-necked ways, and they had been led into exile. The return from exile had begun, but the glory had not yet returned. God's prophet reminded the people that this as-yet-unfulfilled promise would be fulfilled, but they must prepare for the Lord's coming. A better priesthood would be needed, one that would minister in the hope of God's promise to dwell among his people.

Conclusion

As we have seen in this chapter, God's declarative word in his benediction is determinative, working in the world around us. That same word also works within us. In this respect, the Aaronic blessing is a word to be believed as much as received. God's pronouncement is trustworthy and can and must be acted upon. God's people should move about the world in faith, believing what God says is true, often in spite of what our eyes tell us, unlike Malachi's priests. Faith means not only believing that God exists, but "that he rewards those who seek him" (Heb. 11:6). Believing the Aaronic blessing means believing divine benevolence is ours and the beatific vision is happening now as well as in the future. This divine benevolence liberates us not only from fear in general, but fear of the powers that threaten to reward or punish us. "There is no fear in love, but perfect love casts out fear" (1 John 4:18). As the psalmist said, "In God I trust; I shall not be afraid. What can man do to me?" (Ps. 56:11). In thanks for God's rescue, that psalmist readily prays,

For you have delivered my soul from death,
    yes, my feet from falling,
that I may walk before [*lit.*, "before the face of"] God
    in the light of life. (Ps. 56:13)

This divine benevolence not only frees us from the powers of this world, but it also frees us *for* others. Living by faith in God's word enables us to do right even when wronged. It is easy to rationalize doing wrong for the sake of self-preservation, but the knowledge of our standing with God liberates us from that temptation and enables us to do good instead (1 Pet. 3:8–17). Note particularly that Jesus's exhortation to turn the other cheek, walk the second mile, and give our cloak (Matt. 5:38–42) is in the context of his nine benedictions of the Sermon on the Mount, which include, "Blessed are you when others revile you . . ." (Matt. 5:11).

My son and I enjoyed watching the television show *Myth-Busters* for a time. The opening sequence of each episode concluded with one of the hosts saying, "I reject your reality and substitute my own." The chaos that ever impinges upon us in life can make it difficult to discern what is real. Add to that the prevailing outlook of expressive individualism where people are fiercely committed to the dogma that their own perception of reality is what is real. Even if we could see everything perfectly and objectively, that perception is not the whole or ultimate picture. There is

an eternal weight of glory beyond all comparison, as we look not to the things that are seen but to the things that are unseen.

For the things that are seen are transient, but the things that are unseen are eternal. (2 Cor. 4:17–18)

This is why life's trials, though excruciating at times, are relative as "light momentary affliction" (2 Cor. 4:17). While the Aaronic blessing is not yet the fullness of the glory of God in the face of Christ and not the fullness of the blessed hope or the beatific vision, it is of the same essence, the same substance. By comprehending the longings that the Aaronic blessing held forth and the substance of what it was, how it is the oil for the lamp of the Psalms' piety, and how it prepares and points to what is to come, the Aaronic blessing is a fountainhead for faith, a spring of life from which we can and must drink. "Ripple," a 1970 song from the Grateful Dead, describes such a spring. The third verse invites those whose cup is empty to fill it from "a fountain that was not made by the hands of men."[9]

We know that all man-made waters are broken cisterns and only God is the fountain of living waters (Jer. 2:13). The Aaronic blessing, as a "little Bible," is a ladle for the life of God's promised presence and blessedness.

For Further Reflection

1. Practice meditating upon and praying each of the lines of the Aaronic blessing individually, and after doing so, pray the whole blessing, for yourself, others, or both. This may be done alone as a spiritual exercise or with others.[10]

---

9   "Ripple," featuring The Grateful Dead, Warner Bros., 1970.

10 Meditating on Scripture or "divine reading" of Scripture (*lectio Divina*) is an ancient practice often forgotten or neglected by Christians today. Two excellent resources

2. Praying the Psalms is a vital practice for the Christian.[11] Choose one of the psalms mentioned in this chapter and, out of your new understanding of the Aaronic blessing as the background, meditate upon and pray that psalm.

3. In a group, discuss ways in which life's challenges dim God's gracious gaze, and share how elements of the Aaronic blessing or its use in the book of Psalms help you walk by faith and not by sight.

---

for learning this ancient discipline are Dietrich Bonhoeffer, *Meditating on the Word* (Lanham, MD: Cowley, 2008), and Eugene Peterson, *Eat This Book: A Conversation in the Art of Spiritual Reading* (Grand Rapids, MI: Eerdmans, 2006).

11   There are many good works on this subject, but an excellent classic resource is Dietrich Bonhoeffer, *Psalms: The Prayerbook of the Bible* (Minneapolis: Fortress, 1974).

3

The Aaronic Blessing in Light of the New Testament

The Christ of the Blessing

AFTER THE PASSING OF MY MOTHER, I came into possession of letters that she and my father wrote when he was in Europe during World War II. They are unremarkable in the sense that they are only a few of the billions of similar letters that crossed the oceans during that time. Yet as individual yellowed pages written in pencil and fountain pen, they are still singularly moving for one particular reason—they express the longing to be together again. There was little real news in those letters, but the desire to come home was always mentioned. They say absence makes the heart grow fonder (as it did in my parents' case), but time and separation can also have the opposite effect.

By the time of Jesus's birth, five hundred years had passed since the Jerusalem temple had been sacked and razed and the Southern Kingdom of Judah deported to Babylon. At that time, according to Ezekiel's vision, the glory of God departed from the temple (Ezek. 10:18; 11:23), meaning the theophanic presence of God was no longer among his people in his temple and served by his priests. Even though a large number of exiles returned and the temple was rebuilt, it was nothing close to the glorious future of restored Israel foretold by the prophets in which Israel prospered as never before and nations brought their wealth and their praise to God on Mount Zion (e.g., Isa. 2; 11:10–12; 25; 56; Zech. 2:4–5). The glorious night visions of Zechariah, which depicted the return of God's glory to a prosperous Jerusalem, rendering final judgment to Israel's oppressors and drawing an innumerable host to God's presence in the temple, were nowhere in sight (Zechariah 1–6). Life under Roman occupation and the self-aggrandizing kingship of Herod, an Edomite, produced diverse outlooks among the Jews, ranging from outright accommodation to revolutionary zeal. Some, like the early characters we meet in Luke's Gospel, were patiently waiting by faith in the temple for salvation to appear (Luke 2:22–38). They ached for God to come once again to his earthly home. The Aaronic blessing, a precious heirloom of Israel's ancient faith, could easily have been regarded as just that—an heirloom. Would God lift up his countenance on his people once again as he had in the past? The answer comes in many ways in the New Testament, but there are two passages in particular that testify that the promise of God's gracious gaze is being fulfilled in Jesus Christ. The first passage is in John's Gospel, and the second is in Paul's second letter to the Corinthians.

1. The Face of God in John's Gospel

Before looking into John's Gospel, it is worth looking back to the Old Testament for context.

Old Testament Background

All four Evangelists depend upon and draw deeply from the Old Testament: Matthew with numerous overt quotations, Luke with his rich interweaving of redemptive history, and Mark with his ubiquitous allusions and intertextualities, but John's reliance upon the Old Testament is unique in this respect. It has been aptly said that John's Gospel is deep enough for elephants to swim and shallow enough for small children to wade. The greatest variable in perceiving the depth of its waters is the reader's awareness of the Old Testament background to John's Gospel. For example, John 1:4 introduces Jesus as "life," which is the "light of men." A reader steeped in the Old Testament will recognize that John isn't simply uniting two abstract concepts of life and light, but that he is invoking the image of the tabernacle and temple lampstand that stood in the Most Holy Place, a symbol of the tree of life that stood in the center of Eden. The golden lampstand was adorned with golden flowers, each holding an oil wick burning with light. An Old Testament awareness reveals that John is referring to the incarnate Word as the true tree of life.

The lampstand is just one of a host of tabernacle/temple imagery in John's prologue. Most prominently Jesus is presented as the glory of God become flesh, "full of grace and truth" (John 1:14). In his becoming flesh, he "dwelt" or "tabernacled" among us (the root meaning of the Greek term for "dwelt" meaning to live in a tent). The reader is transported to the foot of Mount Sinai and back again to see Jesus as the new tabernacle in which the glory of God has become present among his people. The phrase "grace and truth," read without that Old Testament background, makes it sound like we now have grace whereas we formerly had law and we now have truth as opposed to some kind of factually incorrect understanding of God, perhaps similar to the religious teachers of Jesus's day. However, John's use of "grace" and "truth" is typically not the opposite of "law" and "false," but rather it is his rendering of a very important Old Testament phrase that came to have special meaning at Sinai.

We recall how Moses interceded for Israel in the golden calf episode (Exodus 32). After he prevailed upon God by appealing to God's reputation (32:11) and insisting that God himself must go with his people, not merely one of his angels (33:12–16), Moses asked God to show him his glory (33:18). God acquiesced to Moses's request with the caveat that "you cannot see my face, for man shall not see me and live" (33:20). God sheltered Moses in the rock as his glory passed by, after which Moses was allowed to look upon God's "back" (33:23). Then we hear what God said as he passed by.

> The LORD passed before him and proclaimed, "The LORD, the LORD, a God merciful and gracious, slow to anger, and abounding in steadfast love and faithfulness, keeping steadfast love for thousands, forgiving iniquity and transgression and sin, but who will by no means clear the guilty, visiting the iniquity of the fathers on the children and the children's children, to the third and the fourth generation." (Ex. 34:6–7)

There are two words in God's recitation that become formulaic for God's gracious presence—"steadfast love" (*chesed*) and "faithfulness" (*emeth*). From then on the phrase "steadfast love and faithfulness" invoked the scene at Sinai when God displayed his glory in the climactic resolution of Moses's encounter with God. Furthermore, the phrase is attached immediately to God's covenant name Yahweh—the name that revealed his very essence (Ex. 3:14–15)—and to his saving power (Ex. 15:2–3). This phrase occurs some eighty-five times in the Old Testament, usually in relation to God's actions to bless, protect, preserve, and forgive his people (e.g., Deut. 7:9; 2 Sam. 2:6; Isa. 16:5; Mic. 7:20). Over fifty times in Psalms, God's "steadfast love and faithfulness" are invoked for confidence, help, and praise, including Psalm 85, which is rife with the themes of the Aaronic blessing:

Steadfast love and faithfulness meet;
righteousness and peace kiss each other. (Ps. 85:10)

In the Greek versions of the Old Testament, these terms are translated using the same Greek words in John 1:14. We should not simply understand that the Word was full of grace as opposed to law and full of truth as opposed to falsehood. By using the "tabernacle" verb with these two nouns to describe the glory of God come to dwell among his people, John is clearly intending to invoke the whole scene when God's glory appeared to Moses. When we read "grace and truth" (1:14, 17) our minds should hear the Old Testament's "steadfast love and faithfulness," the character of God who keeps his covenant even with covenant breakers. The God, who promised his glorious and gracious presence through his servant Aaron and Aaron's descendants and whose face was hidden during the days of exile, is shining his face once again through the Word become flesh.

God's Glory in Christ

Though the law was given through Moses (John 1:17), God was a god of grace and truth in the time of the law. When John tells us that "grace and truth" came through Jesus Christ, John is not announcing a new way of God's dealing with people, but rather John is announcing God's arrival in the person of Jesus Christ through whom the fullness of God's grace will be revealed. This one Jesus Christ is the God of glory. Until now, no one could see God and live. Yet the man Jesus Christ, unlike Moses sheltered in the cleft of the rock, is the one who is both the glory of God and come from "the Father's side" (1:18; *lit.*, "in the bosom of the Father"). The overpowering glory of Sinai that Moses had longed to see is manifested in a man, Jesus Christ. John is telling his readers that divine glory, the glory that caused the people of Israel to shrink back from Mount Sinai and plead for Moses to hear God in their stead (Deut. 5:22–27), that divine presence that was so glorious that even Moses could not look upon it directly, is now more fully revealed in the carpenter from Nazareth than on the mountain. In a word, John is telling us that servant glory is greater than Sinai glory. This is the "great parabola," which Paul traces out in Philippians 2:5–11:

> Have this mind among yourselves, which is yours in Christ Jesus, who, though he was in the form of God, did not count equality with God a thing to be grasped, but emptied himself,

by taking the form of a servant, being born in the likeness of men. And being found in human form, he humbled himself by becoming obedient to the point of death, even death on a cross. Therefore God has highly exalted him and bestowed on him the name that is above every name, so that at the name of Jesus every knee should bow, in heaven and on earth and under the earth, and every tongue confess that Jesus Christ is Lord, to the glory of God the Father.

The counterintuitive nature of God's self-revelation in the humility of the incarnation will be at the heart of Jesus's conflict with the religious authorities, and yet it is what makes the glory of God in Christ transcend all previous manifestations of God's glory.

Competing Glories

The prominence of God's glory in John 1:14 along with the frequent mention of glory through John's Gospel highlights a clear two-phase structure to the book as it pertains to the theme of seeing God's glory. Many have designated the two parts the "book of signs" and the "book of glory." However, glory is a prominent theme in the first half as well as the second. For the first eleven chapters, John describes a competition of glories. There is the glory that comes from God and the glory that comes from man (John 5:41, 44; 7:18). Jesus did not seek his own glory (8:50), but his signs manifested the glory that was given him by God (2:11). Jesus's authority came from God who sent him, while those who speak on their own authority seek their own glory (7:18). It was the Father who glorified the Son (8:54), and that glory is seen by believing in the Son's witness (11:40). Jesus appealed to the testimonies of Moses and Isaiah, who had testified to his glory on Mount Sinai and in the temple, respectively (12:41, 46).[1] This glory will be climactically revealed at "the hour," a phrase Jesus uses to describe the time of his crucifixion (2:4; 7:30; 8:20; 12:27).[2] The irony of servant glory being the greater glory climaxes in the idea of glorification as crucifixion.

> This is the whole message of the Gospel of John—the glory of God, which is the glory of Christ, manifest among men. For twelve chapters John shows that glory diffuse, as it were: manifest in sign and word; for nine he shows the glory focused [sic]: concentrated in the keenness of a love that loved to the end (John 13:1).[3]

The Light in Battle against Darkness

These competing glories, the glory that comes from God and the glory that comes from man, play out in John's Gospel as a battle between the light and the darkness. John, in something of a "spoiler alert," tells us this in his prologue. "The light shines in

---

1   As noted before, it was the glory of God in which Moses stood on Mount Sinai, that he encountered in the Tent of Meeting and saw as it passed by while he was sheltered in the cleft of the rock.

2   Our translations at times can be confusing. In some instances "the hour" is obscured because the possessive pronoun obscures the definite article "the," which is not translated (John 2:4). In other cases, translations add the "the" when Jesus is not referring to the hour of his crucifixion but to a different hour (John 4:21, 23).

3   Karl T. Cooper, "The Best Wine: John 2:1–11" *Westminster Theological Journal* 41, no. 2 (1979), 364. What follows concerning the motifs of light and darkness are from his unpublished Gospels lectures delivered at Covenant Theological Seminary, circa Fall 1985.

the darkness, and the darkness has not overcome it" (1:5). This battle is only resolved through conflict and, for a time, remains in doubt. When Judas went out to betray Jesus at the Last Supper, John observes, "And it was night" (John 13:30). From that point on in John's Gospel, at least on a literary level, darkness prevails. Jesus's arrest and trial, Peter's betrayal, Mary's early morning visit to the tomb, and the disciples' night-long fishing expedition all take place in darkness. Even Jesus's appearances to the disciples were in the evening or behind closed doors (20:19, 26). It is not until we see Jesus standing on the shore of the Sea of Tiberias that we are told that day is breaking (21:4). As he gives fishing directions to the once-and-again fishermen (21:4–6), the great fish harvest, foretold long ago in Ezekiel's temple vision (Ezek. 47:10–12), exposes the identity of the man on the shore. Peter, having dragged the net ashore, sees Jesus kneeling by the very kind of charcoal fire whose flicker exposed the betraying face of Peter in Caiaphas's courtyard (21:9; cf. 18:18). The light truly overcame the darkness just as John had testified at the beginning of his Gospel, and so in the broad light of day Peter receives a threefold commission from Jesus despite his earlier threefold denial (21:15–19).

"He Who Has Seen Me Has Seen the Father"

John is resolved to bear witness—to testify—that the glory of God, which had marked God's presence among his people in the days of Moses and the tabernacle throughout Israel's history until the exile, and been sealed in the Aaronic blessing, has now been revealed in the humble person of the incarnate Son of God. John is not content simply to relate the facts of Jesus's life, but wants the reader to "see." Seeing in John's Gospel is the vital basis for bearing witness about God (1:14, 18, 34; 3:11, 32; 6:46; 8:38; 20:18, 25). Jesus has seen God and has come to bear witness. Though we have never seen God, the Father sent the Son, who has come from the very presence of God, to bear witness to glory of the Father (1:14; 17:5). But Jesus is more than a witness to the Father. "Whoever has seen me has seen the Father" (14:9). To have looked upon Christ in his earthly ministry is to have looked upon the Father himself, if not in his essence, in his reflected glory.

As Jesus approached the climactic glory of the crucifixion, he prayed for his followers. The glory that the Son shared with the Father before the incarnation is the glory that the Son petitions for his followers (17:22). As the one who had come from the Father's "bosom," (1:18)—not from the "back," which Moses had seen, but from before the face of God—and who would soon return (16:5, 10, 17, 28; 17:11, 13), the Son asked the Father that his followers would be with him to behold his glory.

> Father, I desire that they also, whom you have given me, may
> be with me where I am, to see my glory that you have given
> me because you loved me before the foundation of the world.
> (17:24)

This glory is derived from the "name" of the Father (17:6, 11, 12), the name that Jesus has made known (17:26). In fact, it is "in the name" that he asks that God would "keep" them (17:11) as Jesus had "kept" them in the Father's name that was given to Jesus (17:12). His followers would remain in the world, however, even as they were with the Son in his exalted state in glory (17:15) for they are to extend the mission of the incarnation as he sends them into the world (17:18). But as they are sent, they are sent as a consecrated people, set apart just as the multitude at the foot of Sinai (17:19).

As the Farewell Discourse (John 14–17) began, Jesus promised, "Peace I leave with you; my peace I give to you. Not as the world gives do I give to you. Let not your hearts be troubled, neither let them be afraid" (14:27). By manifesting the glory of God in the flesh, laying down his life for his sheep, taking it up again in the resurrection, returning to the Father, and sending the Spirit, Jesus assumes the priesthood of the Aaronic blessing, securing for his followers shalom, which is life. By his testimony, John bears witness to Christ so that we might believe, and by believing, have life in his name (20:31).

All of this is to show that in a systematic way John's Gospel bears witness to how the Aaronic blessing is secured in Christ for his followers and promised to those who through their testimony would also believe. "Jesus said to him, 'Have you believed because you have seen me? Blessed are those who have not seen and yet have believed'" (20:29). To believe in the Jesus of John's witness is to stand under the gracious gaze of God.

2. The Face of God according to Paul (2 Corinthians 3–4)

The connections between the Aaronic blessing and John's Gospel, while expansive, are based on thematic rather than explicit connections. Paul in 2 Corinthians 3–4 is explicit in connecting the glory of God, the shining face of Moses, and the person and work of Christ. In his letter, Paul upbraids the church at

Corinth for having been influenced by what he sarcastically calls "super-apostles" (11:5; 12:11). Those false apostles (11:13) had demeaned Paul's ministry because he was not as eloquent as they (11:6) and because of the struggles under which Paul carried out his ministry. Paul not only responds by pointing out that his hardships were on account of the Corinthians but that his suffering bore the very marks of Jesus himself (13:4). Similar to what we have seen in John's Gospel, Paul is encountering the conflict, the inherent incompatibility, of the glory that comes from God and the glory that man gives. The glory of Christ, being the very glory of God, is the only meaningful and lasting glory, but it comes through suffering. This is the larger context in which Paul takes up the subject of the faces of Moses and Christ in 2 Corinthians 3–4.

Paul's sufficiency as God's apostle is that he is a minister of the new covenant not of the old (3:6). The superiority of this ministry can be seen in the fading glory of Moses's face as recounted in Exodus 34:29–35. After Moses had received the law from God, his face shone with the glory of God such that the people were afraid to come near him (34:30). So Moses, after speaking, placed a veil over his face to quash their fears (34:33). Verses 34–35 go on to relate how this became Moses's custom whenever he met with God in the tent of meeting. Eventually Moses's face would cease to shine, and he could remove the veil. Paul attributes the fading of Moses's face to the passing nature of the old covenant. The glory that Moses reflected didn't last (2 Cor. 3:7). The fading glory meant that the old covenant couldn't fully secure the faithful's standing before God, but could only serve as a "ministry of condemnation" (3:9).

On the other hand, the ministry of the new covenant, being a ministry of the Spirit, secures and ensures the abiding presence of God because it constitutes a "ministry of righteousness" (3:9). Therefore, the glory of Christ surpasses the glory of the old covenant (3:10).

Indeed, in this case, what once had glory has come to have no glory at all, because of the glory that surpasses it. For if what was being brought to an end came with glory, much more will what is permanent have glory. (3:10–11)

Those who, out of unbelief, refuse to turn from the fading glory of Moses to the unfading glory of the new covenant remain spiritually blind. However,

But when one turns to the Lord, the veil is removed. Now the Lord is the Spirit, and where the Spirit of the Lord is, there is freedom. And we all, with unveiled face, beholding the glory of the Lord, are being transformed into the same image from one degree of glory to another. For this comes from the Lord who is the Spirit. (3:16–18)

There was glory under the old covenant, even though it could never fully confirm God's people in righteousness and even though that glory faded (3:9). The glory of the new covenant is not a different glory but in greater proportion and duration through the work and presence of the Spirit (3:8). The administration of that glory under the old covenant was intended to expire when superseded by the permanence of the new covenant (3:11). This new stage of glory is a glory on which we can now look with unveiled faces because it is unfading, the destiny of those who turn to the Lord (3:16, 18). The glory that was espied from the foot of Mount Sinai, descended upon the tabernacle, was shown in Moses's face, and pronounced with the raised hands of Aaron is the now-and-future visage of those who have turned to the Lord. We now behold the glory of the Lord and, in doing so, are being transformed into the same image.

For Paul this exonerated his outwardly less glorious ministry over that of the "super-apostles" because his was informed by the glory of God (4:1–2). Those who see it otherwise are "blinded" because they can't see through the veil of Christlike suffering (4:4). Paul's *apologia* for his ministry concludes by locating the source of this transforming glory. It is no less than the glory of the Creator, the God who said, "Let light shine out of darkness" (4:6; cf. Gen. 1:3). He is the one robed in light (Ps. 104:2) and in whose light we see light because he is the fountain of life (Ps. 36:9). It is the light of this knowledge through which we now behold the glory of God in the face of Jesus Christ.

The glory of the incarnation is glorious, but it is even greater when we see it in the context of Paul's vindication of his ministry. The reasons others were diminishing Paul's ministry pertained to the lowliness, shabbiness, struggles, and hardships Paul was experiencing as well as Paul's unadorned rhetoric. Paul's defense was that his ministry bore the marks of the ministry of Christ himself. Just as in 1 Corinthians Paul had asserted that the life of the church at Corinth should conform to the nature and pattern of Christ's death on the cross (1 Cor. 1:10–17), in 2 Corinthians he similarly asserts the superiority of his ministry because it conforms to the shape of the cross.

New Testament theologian John Barclay, in a larger treatment of the nature of the cross in the Greco-Roman world *vis-à-vis* 1 Corinthians 1–4, has said,

> The wisdom of the cross is not just an alternative wisdom but an anti-wisdom. . . . God's election does not simply bypass the wise and powerful: it shames them by an act that confounds the normal ranking of status or honor.[4]

As a social framework in which the weakest and the least honored by society would be the most essential and most honored (1 Cor. 12:22–23), the church is to faithfully reflect the nature of God's action in Christ that brought the church into being *ex nihilo* (1 Cor. 1:28). It is altogether fitting, and even necessary, that a true apostle of the cross would follow the shape of this same cruciformity. It is to this very necessity Paul directly moves after drawing the arc from the light of the Creator to the face of the Redeemer:

> But we have this treasure in jars of clay, to show that the surpassing power belongs to God and not to us. We are afflicted in every way, but not crushed; perplexed, but not driven to despair; persecuted, but not forsaken; struck down, but not destroyed; always carrying in the body the death of Jesus, so that the life of Jesus may also be manifested in our bodies. For we who live are always being given over to death for Jesus' sake,

4   John M. G. Barclay, "Crucifixion as Wisdom: Exploring the Ideology of a Disreputable Social Movement," *The Wisdom and Foolishness of God*, eds. Christophe Chalamet and Hans-Christoph Askani (Minneapolis: Fortress Press, 2015), 5.

so that the life of Jesus also may be manifested in our mortal flesh. So death is at work in us, but life in you. (2 Cor. 4:7–12)

This move by Paul to exonerate his apostolicity by its humble form takes its place alongside John's witness to the greater glory being incarnate and crucified glory. Both say the same thing in similar ways. The image of the shining face of God, as glorious as it was under the old covenant, has been manifested in a decisive, climactic, and transformative way in Jesus Christ. Jesus's religious critics and Paul's "super-apostles" (2 Cor. 11:5) were what Martin Luther terms "theologians of glory." In Luther's "Heidelberg Disputations," he writes, "He deserves to be called a theologian, however, who comprehends the visible and manifest things of God seen through suffering and the cross."[5] In the proof of this disputation, Luther adds:

> The manifest and visible things of God are placed in opposition to the invisible, namely, his human nature, weakness, foolishness. The Apostle in I Cor. 1[:25] calls them the weakness and folly of God. Because men misused the knowledge of God through works, God wished again to be recognized in suffering, and to condemn wisdom concerning invisible things by means of wisdom concerning visible things, so that those who did not honor God as manifested in His works should honor him as he is hidden in his suffering. As the Apostle says in 1 Cor 1[:21], "For since, in the wisdom of God, the world did not know God through wisdom, it pleased God through the folly of what

5   "Heidelberg Disputations," *Luther's Works, Vol. 31: Career of the Reformer: I*, ed. Harold J. Grimm (Philadelphia, PA: Muhlenberg, 1957), 40.

we preach to save those who believe." Now it is not sufficient for anyone, and it does him no good to recognize God in his glory and majesty, unless he recognizes him in the humility and shame of the cross. Thus God destroys the wisdom of the wise, as Isa. 45[:15] says, "Truly, Thou art a God who hidest Thyself."

So, also, in John 14[:8], where Philip spoke according to the theology of glory: "Show us the Father." Christ forthwith set aside his flighty thought about seeking God elsewhere and led him to himself, saying, "Philip, he who has seen Me has seen the Father" [John 14:9]. For this reason true theology and recognition of God are in the crucified Christ, as it is also stated in John 10 [John 14:6]: "No one comes to the Father, but by Me." "I am the door" [John 10:9], and so forth.[6]

In the German, the word *visible* is literally "back parts," a clear allusion to Exodus 33:23 when God limited Moses's vision of God's glory. The favorable countenance of God pronounced in Numbers 6:22–27 finds its full expression and realization in Jesus Christ, the glory become flesh (John 1:14), in whose face we see the glory of God (2 Cor. 3:18). The glory in his face is the unfading glory of the gospel (2 Cor. 3:7–11). Whoever has seen the Son has seen the Father (John 14:9), therefore believing in the Son as the ultimate fulfillment of the benediction is the only avenue to its blessings.

The high priestly prayer of John's Gospel reveals that Jesus was assuming the Aaronic role of priestly benediction. Paul shows that Jesus assumes the glory-reflecting role of Moses. Together

---

6 Luther, "Heidelberg Disputation," 52–53.

they demonstrate that Jesus Christ is the full revelation of the beatific countenance of the Aaronic blessing. This fullness is found not just in the incarnation, but in Christ's death, burial, resurrection, and ascension. As the author of Hebrews declares, "He is the radiance of the glory of God and the exact imprint of his nature," as well as the one who "upholds the universe by the word of his power" (Heb. 1:3). All God's promises find their "yes" in Christ (2 Cor. 1:20). Among the promises answered in Christ is the great benediction of Israel, that word spoken over Israel for fifteen centuries, the Aaronic blessing. What does the lifted countenance of God blessing his people look like? It looks like God the Son

> manifested in the flesh,
>> vindicated by the Spirit,
>>> seen by angels,
> proclaimed among the nations,
>> believed on in the world,
>>> taken up in glory. (1 Tim. 3:16)

For Further Discussion

1. Why is "servant glory" greater than Sinai glory?

2. What are the ways you feel the tension between the glory that comes from other people and the glory that comes only from God?

3. How does Christ's high priestly prayer give us intimate access to what the Aaronic blessing offers?

4. Peter calls Christians to rejoice "insofar as you share Christ's sufferings" (1 Pet. 4:13). Among the things to which Paul aspires is that he "may share [Christ's] sufferings" (Phil. 3:10). Read and reflect upon both statements in their context. What does the scandal of Christ's cross ask of Christ's followers?

4

The Aaronic Blessing and Me

The Consequences of the Blessing
Part 1—Just Look at Yourself

IN NATHANIEL HAWTHORNE'S SHORT STORY "The Minister's Black Veil," the young Reverend Mr. Hooper unexplainably arrived for Sabbath worship wearing a black crepe veil covering all but his mouth. One old woman remarked, "I don't like it. He has changed himself into something awful, only by hiding his face."[1] As Mr. Hooper ascended the pulpit to carry out his ministerial duties, the veil "shook with his measured breath, as he gave out the psalm; it threw its obscurity between him and the holy page, as he read the Scriptures; and while he prayed, the veil lay heavily on his uplifted countenance. Did he seek to hide it from the dread Being whom he was addressing?"[2] He had been a good though

---

1 Nathaniel Hawthorne, "The Minister's Black Veil: A Parable," *Twice Told Tales in Two Volumes* (Boston: Ticknor, Reed, and Fields, 1853), 1:47–66.

2 Hawthorne, "The Minister's Black Veil," 49–50.

THE AARONIC BLESSING AND ME

not energetic preacher before, but his sermon that day on secret sin carried a peculiar power such that some wondered if it was the same man. Subsequently, speculations abounded about the reason for the unexplained veil. The minister continued for some time to carry out his duties with the dark veil, whether funerals or weddings, and thus a darker mystery formed between him and the people of his congregation, with the people afraid to ask his reason for the veil.

At first, Hooper's fiancé, Elizabeth, didn't mind the veil. "There is nothing terrible in this piece of crape, except that it hides a face which I am always glad to look upon."[3] Yet when he refused to remove the veil even for her, the pall that came upon everyone else fell upon her as well. Whenever he went out in the village, he cast a dark shadow. He even refused to look at himself in a mirror or stoop to drink from a reflective fountain. While a sorrowful darkness remained on him, it did have the effect of making him "a very efficient clergyman."[4] "He became a man of awful power over souls that were in agony for sin. His converts always regarded him with a dread peculiar to themselves, affirming, though but figuratively, that, before he brought them to celestial light, they had been with him behind the black veil."[5] In fact, he became so widely known that he ministered at the funerals of so many that he had "one congregation in the church, and a more crowded one in the churchyard."[6]

Even as he lay upon his deathbed he refused to remove the veil.

3 Hawthorne, "The Minister's Black Veil," 57.
4 Hawthorne, "The Minister's Black Veil," 57.
5 Hawthorne, "The Minister's Black Veil," 61.
6 Hawthorne, "The Minister's Black Veil," 62.

All through his life that piece of crape had hung between him and the world: it had separated him from cheerful brotherhood and woman's love, and kept him in the saddest of all prisons, his own heart; and still it lay upon his face, as if to deepen the gloom of his darksome chamber, and shade him from the sunshine of eternity.[7]

Mr. Hooper insisted on wearing the veil to his grave, with his dying words his final sermon:

Why do you tremble at me alone? . . . Tremble also at each other! . . . When the friend shows his inmost heart to his friend; the lover to his best beloved; when man does not vainly shrink from the eye of his Creator, loathsomely treasuring up the secret of his sin; then deem me a monster, for the symbol beneath which I have lived, and die![8]

If not plain before, his dying declaration explained the symbol. Until acknowledged and expiated, there is a black veil upon every human heart. The fear and loathing that the veil had unexplainedly produced in others was not toward the universally esteemed Mr. Hooper, but toward one's own soul under the "celestial light" of God's gaze.

Similar to Mr. Hooper, the visage of Christ should cause us all to look at ourselves in its light. As we do, we will look upon ourselves differently. We are to see our own black veil, but also see the light of divine favor, the uplifted countenance of God. A

7   Hawthorne, "The Minister's Black Veil," 63.
8   Hawthorne, "The Minister's Black Veil," 65.

different veil has been removed, the veil of the old covenant. Now by the Spirit we see the unfading glory of the face of God in Christ, which holds forth all the benefits of God's saving. Regeneration, repentance and faith, justification, adoption, sanctification, and glorification all bear a relationship to the standing that this vision signifies. It signifies that now we are able to stand in God's presence, blameless with great joy (Jude 24–25). It signifies our transformation. "And we all, with unveiled face, beholding the glory of the Lord, are being transformed into the same image from one degree of glory to another" (2 Cor. 3:18). It signifies our final glorification. "For now we see in a mirror dimly, but then face to face. Now I know in part; then I shall know fully, even as I have been fully known" (1 Cor. 13:12).

While the grace of the Aaronic blessing was administered under the period of the law, it was constrained by the fading glory that Moses's veil obscured. The fading nature was not due to any defect in God's benevolence, but to the law's inability to "perfect the conscience of the worshiper" (Heb. 9:9). Even with the "ink" of covenant renewal fresh on the pages of Deuteronomy, Moses acknowledged that "to this day the LORD has not given you a heart to understand or eyes to see or ears to hear" (Deut. 29:4). While the sacrifices, types, and ordinances of the old covenant were "sufficient and efficacious" to administer the covenant of grace for that time, they themselves pointed ultimately to what God would do in Christ.[9] As the writer of Hebrews said, "It is impossible for the blood of bulls and goats to take away sins" (Heb. 10:4). As the "mediator of a new covenant" (Heb. 9:15),

---

9   *Westminster Confession of Faith and Catechisms,* PCA ed. (Atlanta, GA: Committee on Discipleship Ministries, 2005), ch. 7, par. 5, p. 32.

Jesus Christ is a better priest (Hebrews 8) in a better tabernacle (Hebrews 9) and offers a better sacrifice (Hebrews 10). This new covenant has made the old obsolete (Heb. 8:13). Unlike Israel who heard the Aaronic blessing pronounced for the first time and whose consecration would not endure long enough to see them through the wilderness, the better ministry of Christ has sanctified those who believe *once for all* (Heb. 10:10).

All that was promised in the Aaronic blessing has been realized and is now administered in its fullness in Jesus Christ. The words of God spoken "at many times and in many ways" have now been spoken finally and fully in Christ, including the word of words of the Aaronic blessing (Heb. 1:1–2). For "when one turns to the Lord, the veil is removed" (2 Cor. 3:16), and this has profound consequences for how we see our standing before God. In the light of the fullness of God's gracious gaze in Christ, we are called to look at ourselves anew in several ways because four "veils" have been removed.

1. The Veil of the Law

First of all, we Christians see a greater glory than under the law. What shone previously is now surpassing in degree and duration. As John Calvin put it,

> This is not a correction of what goes before, but rather a confirmation; for he [Paul] means that the glory of the law is extinguished when the gospel comes forth. As the moon and stars, though in themselves they are not merely luminous, but diffuse their light over the whole earth, do, nevertheless, disappear before the brightness of the sun; so however glorious the

law was in itself, it has, nevertheless, no glory in comparison with the excellence of the gospel.[10]

Here Calvin uses the word "law" not to refer to the commands of God, but to the period of time or economy from the Mosaic covenant until the coming of Christ. The glory of God that shone upon Israel through the pronouncement of the Aaronic blessing was only a portion of the glory of God that now shines in the face of Christ. Though Moses's face shone with the glory of God from the face-to-face meeting with God, Moses's face was only a token or a shadow of the true glory that is manifested in Christ. The veil that obscured the fading nature of this glory is now removed by Christ and in Christ, who is the very image of God.

Peter, speaking of the prophets of the Old Testament, wrote,

It was revealed to them that they were serving not themselves but you, in the things that have now been announced to you through those who preached the good news to you by the Holy Spirit sent from heaven, things into which angels long to look. (1 Pet. 1:12)

Though those Spirit-inspired prophets wrote of Christ who was to come, predicting "the sufferings of Christ and the subsequent glories" (1:11), preachers of the new covenant revealed "things into which angels long to look" (1:12). In other words, as we saw previously from John 1:18, in Jesus a glory is revealed that is beyond anything in the Old Testament. What makes this glory

10 John Calvin, *Commentary on the Second Epistle to the Corinthians*, vol. 2, trans. John Pringle (Grand Rapids, MI: Baker, 1984), 179.

greater is that it is gospel glory, the glory that is revealed through the death, burial, and resurrection of Jesus. As John wrote, it was only after Christ's suffering, his "glorification," that even the disciples fully grasped who Jesus was and what he did (John 12:16).

We see even better than the eyewitnesses to Jesus, because we have the light of the resurrection and the Spirit-inspired testimony of Scripture. We mustn't envy the eyewitnesses for their "ringside seat." Through their inspired testimony, we see more than what they saw as the events of the Gospels were unfolding. At Sinai, even though the spectacular sight of fire engulfed the mountaintop, Israel "heard the sound of words, but saw no form; there was only a voice" (Deut. 4:12). In the second commandment God forbade making of images of him (Deut. 5:8) because when it comes to knowing God, the ear "sees" more than the eye. We see more of Jesus than the eyewitnesses once did because we see through their testimony. As Jesus said to Thomas, "Have you believed because you have seen me? Blessed are those who have not seen and yet have believed" (John 20:29).

In the Old Testament, the visible glory of God is often correlated with the Spirit of God.[11] Therefore, the glory of God is not only manifested in the person and work of Christ, but also in Christ's sending the Spirit to dwell in us and us in him. In telling the Samaritan woman that the hour had come when all would worship in Spirit and truth, Jesus was announcing the Spirit as the successor to any and all stone temples (John 4:23).[12] Descending

---

11 For more on this rich thematic correlation, see Meredith G. Kline, *Images of the Spirit* (South Hamilton, MA: Meredith G. Kline, 1986).

12 For making the case that Jesus is referring to the Holy Spirit, see Herman Ridderbos, *The Gospel of John* (Grand Rapids, MI: Eerdmans, 1997), 163–64.

upon the church at Pentecost, the Spirit constitutes the presence of the ascended Christ on earth (Matt. 28:20) and the return of the glory that had departed from the temple in the days of exile. Jesus promised that the Spirit would guide his followers in the truth (John 14:15–17; 16:13) and glorify the Son (John 16:14). The Spirit has done so by removing the veil of the law to reveal the glory of the Son through the external witness of Pentecost and by indwelling believers. Notably, in promising to send the Spirit, Jesus pronounced a benediction on his followers in saying, "Peace I leave with you; my peace I give to you" (John 14:27). In the very act of imparting the Spirit to his followers, Jesus said, "Peace be with you" twice (John 20:19, 21) and then again when truant Thomas was present (20:26). The Spirit is present and participates in bestowing the shalom of the Aaronic blessing by removing the veil of the old covenant so that, like Peter, James, and John on the Mount of Transfiguration, we see Jesus in glory (Matt. 17:1–8; Mark 9:2–8; Luke 9:28–36). Through the Father's sending of the Son, the work of the Son, and the application by the Spirit, we behold the glory of God in the face of Jesus Christ.

2. The Veil of Old Debts

In addition to the veil of the old covenant, another veil that is lifted is the veil of our sin that stood between us and God.

> And you, who were dead in your trespasses and the uncircumcision of your flesh, God made alive together with him, having forgiven us all our trespasses, by canceling the record of debt that stood against us with its legal demands. This he set aside, nailing it to the cross. (Col. 2:13–14)

Mr. Hooper's black veil is lifted. Just as Israel's redemption and consecration preceded the Aaronic blessing, so seeing the glory of God in the face of Jesus Christ requires that we must first be made holy and blameless. The psalmist asked:

> Who shall ascend the hill of the LORD?
>   And who shall stand in his holy place?
> He who has clean hands and a pure heart,
>   who does not lift up his soul to what is false
> and does not swear deceitfully. (Ps. 24:3–4)

Under conviction of sin, David's prayer for God's mercy appealed to God's "steadfast love" (Ps. 51:1), God's *chesed* expressed in the covenantal Aaronic blessing. It was before God's "eyes" that David had sinned (51:4). He pled, "Hide your face from my sins, and blot out all my iniquities" (51:9), that he would not be cast away from God's "presence," which, remember, is literally "face" (51:11). David's prayer that God would "restore" to David the joy of God's salvation is literally "send from your face" (51:12). David knew that such joy came only from the presence or face of God. Yet the putrefaction of sin, as symbolized in Levitical laws concerning uncleanness, breached the social bond between God and his people. Just as Adam and Eve hid from the face of God because of the knowledge of their shame, all people who become sentient to their sin hide their faces from God. This hiding takes many forms, from the seared conscience of utter denial of God's existence to the inconsolable grief of the ravaged conscience. Lady MacBeth's "damn spot" will not wash out without divine ablution.

That absolution, provided typologically in the sacrificial system of the Mosaic Law, has been realized in Christ's "ministry of reconciliation" and has been proclaimed by Paul in the "message of reconciliation" (2 Cor. 5:18).

That is, in Christ God was reconciling the world to himself, not counting their trespasses against them, and entrusting to us the message of reconciliation. Therefore, we are ambassadors for Christ, God making his appeal through us. We implore you on behalf of Christ, be reconciled to God. For our sake he made him to be sin who knew no sin, so that in him we might become the righteousness of God. (2 Cor. 5:19–21)

As the hymn says, "Arise, my soul, arise, / shake off your guilty fears" because "before the throne my surety stands."[13] The death of Christ has atoned for sin, bearing away both actual guilt and shame so that "there is therefore now no condemnation for those who are in Christ Jesus" (Rom. 8:1). God is able "to keep you from stumbling and to present you blameless before the presence of his glory with great joy" (Jude 24). The acme of fellowship with God, to stand in his presence and behold his beaming countenance, is ours now by grace through faith in Christ.

3. The Veil of Our Old Nature

Standing in the light of the glory of God reflected in the face of Christ also enables us to see ourselves more clearly in a reconciled and restored status before God. Our improved sight also enables

---

13 Charles Wesley, "Arise, My Soul, Arise," *Trinity Hymnal*, rev. ed. (Atlanta: Great Commission Publications, 1997), no. 305.

us to see the reality of our sin. Our blindness to the indwelling sin that continues to exert a power over us in spite of our pardon is another veil that is removed in the light of God's countenance. There are two distinct though related aspects of this freedom from sin's power. The first is repentance.

The grace of repentance is nowhere taught so straightforwardly as in 2 Corinthians 7, a passage that follows Paul's words about the veil of the law being lifted in chapters 3–4. In response to what has been called Paul's "severe letter," a letter that we do not have, the believers at Corinth responded to Paul's rebuke with "godly grief" (7:9) and not "worldly grief" (7:10). Termed by the Westminster Shorter Catechism as "repentance unto life," the answer to Question 87 defines this as

> a saving grace, whereby a sinner, out of a true sense of his sin, and apprehension of the mercy of God in Christ, doth, with grief and hatred of his sin, turn from it unto God, with full purpose of, and endeavor after, new obedience.[14]

In the light of the fading glory of the old covenant, the law, like the blood of righteous Abel (Heb. 12:24), could only condemn. The glory of the new covenant in the pardoning blood of Christ means that our sin is not a death sentence. The light of the gospel, as the light of God's word, exposes our sins and sinful condition as it shines in our hearts. Knowing that those sins have already been laid on Christ, we can willingly and eagerly acknowledge them (Rom. 8:1). The first of Luther's "Ninety-Five Theses" proposed

---

14 *Westminster Confession of Faith and Catechisms*, 395.

that "when our Lord and Master Jesus Christ said, 'Repent,' he willed the entire life of believers to be one of repentance."[15]

Looking upon the glory of God in the face of Christ enables godly sorrow in two ways. It enables us to look upon the face of Christ to be reminded of our sinful condition in general as well as reminded of particular sins. When we look upon Christ, his righteous life and his resurrection vindication (1 Tim. 3:16), the Spirit shines a light on us so that we are made aware in new and deeper ways of our need for God's grace. Looking on Christ also enables us to see how he stood in our place for our sin. In the light of both our sinful condition and the perfections of Christ, faith sees the way back, which godly sorrow provides, rather than the dead end of worldly sorrow.

> If you, O LORD, should mark iniquities,
>   O Lord, who could stand?
> But with you there is forgiveness,
>   that you may be feared. (Ps. 130:3–4)

This is cause for joy (Jude 24–25), as Christian sang in *Pilgrim's Progress*:

> Thus far did I come laden with my Sin
> Nor could ought ease the grief that I was in,
> Till I came hither: What a place is this!
> Must here be the beginning of my bliss?

15 Martin Luther, "Ninety-Five Theses or Disputation on the Power and Efficacy of Indulgences," *Luther's Works, Vol. 31: Career of the Reformer: I*, ed. Harold J. Grimm (Philadelphia, PA: Muhlenberg, 1957), 25.

THE CONSEQUENCES OF THE BLESSING, PART I

Must here the Burden fall from off my back?
Must here the strings that bound it to me crack?
Blest Cross! Blest Sepulchre! Blest rather be
The Man that there was put to Shame for me![16]

So our grief and hatred is of our sin and old nature not of ourselves. Godly sorrow also involves "turning from" or turning around, a change of mind. This determination to change leads to mortification, the second aspect of the freedom that comes from the glory of Christ. Mortification is putting to death the old sin nature that continues to abide in us. "For if you live according to the flesh you will die, but if by the Spirit you put to death the deeds of the body, you will live" (Rom. 8:13). While "flesh" sometimes refers simply to our physical bodies, at other times the word describes the fallen human nature that remains in us once we have been born again with a new nature (Rom. 7:5, 14, 18, 25). While we are made new by the regenerating work of the Spirit (2 Cor. 5:17; Titus 3:5), this old nature still exists alongside the new. We are one person with two natures. The process of Christian maturity, of sanctification, involves putting to death that old nature and nurturing the new nature, "mortification and vivification." In Romans 8, Paul describes the outcome of this process as being "conformed to the image of his Son" (8:29). In 2 Corinthians 4, he describes this whole process in terms of God's gracious gaze through Christ.

Now the Lord is the Spirit, and where the Spirit of the Lord is, there is freedom. And we all, with unveiled face, beholding the

---

16 John Bunyan, *The Pilgrim's Progress from This World to That Which Is to Come* (Carlisle, PA: Banner of Truth, 1977), 36.

glory of the Lord, are being transformed into the same image from one degree of glory to another. For this comes from the Lord who is the Spirit. (2 Cor. 3:17–18)

The end goal of Christian discipleship—becoming like Christ—happens in this life through the process of gazing upon or contemplating God's glory in the face of Christ. When we contemplate Christ, we see what we will one day be, and by contemplating him, we undergo God's transformation, both in conforming us to his likeness and purging the dross. God's gracious gaze in Christ provides us what the Aaronic blessing could not under the law but can now provide under the gospel because the Spirit illumines and indwells us.

The glory of God in the face of Christ reflects God's gracious gaze on us, but it reflects it *as* us, as people created in the same divine image as the human nature of Christ. As the apostle John wrote:

Beloved, we are God's children now, and what we will be has not yet appeared; but we know that when he appears we shall be like him, because we shall see him as he is. And everyone who thus hopes in him purifies himself as he is pure. (1 John 3:2–3)

John doesn't mean that Christ has not yet appeared, for besides being an eyewitness himself, John begins 1 John by saying he is testifying to what he has seen (1 John 1:1). It is our being like Christ that has not yet appeared.

Diet and exercise promotionals abound with "before and after" pictures showing a person before the rigors and disciplines involved and then after with the transformative results. What is superior about the transformative power of seeing the glory of God in the face of Christ is that we see our end result even as we still aspire to it. This process of transformation is both agonizing and joyful. Since our old nature is part of who we are, it has a survival instinct and doesn't die easily. Yet our growing freedom from sin, becoming more and more like Christ and keeping God's commands, is a source of joy and satisfaction. The psalmist envisioned this as he confessed, "As for me, I shall behold your face in righteousness; when I awake, I shall be satisfied with your likeness" (Ps. 17:15).

We see this process dramatized in C. S. Lewis's *The Voyage of the Dawn Treader*, the third-published of The Chronicles of Narnia. Eustace Scrubb was an unwilling companion on the epic voyage of Narnian Prince Caspian, and the priggish boy missed no opportunity to make the lives of his fellow voyagers miserable. When their ship landed at a remote island to make repairs, Eustace wandered off to avoid the work and find a more comfortable place to sleep. When he happened upon a cave containing an old dragon's hoard, he fell asleep on the heaps of gold and jewels with one of the many golden armlets on his arm. Waking, he discovered that he had been turned into a dragon himself through the lingering magic of the now-excruciatingly-tight armlet. While his appearance to his companions naturally terrified them at first, they eventually realized the dragon was Eustace. The painful armlet, his general misery, and the kindness with which his friends treated him humbled him mightily. As a dragon, he actually became helpful in the work of ship repairs and generally a much more pleasant Eustace than he had been before. But he was still a dragon, and as time for the ship's departure drew near, he was faced with the prospect of being left behind. Then suddenly he appeared to the ship's company as a boy once again. How? Everyone wanted to know.

According to Eustace, the majestic lion Aslan had appeared to him and led him to a mountain pool. Without words, the lion told Eustace to wash himself and, as he did, Eustace was ecstatic to discover that the dragon scales fell off with scrubbing. His joy was only momentary when he saw that underneath the layer he'd just scrubbed off was another layer of dragon skin. After several attempts with the same result, Eustace related:

> Then the lion said—but I don't know if it spoke—You will have to let me undress you. I was afraid of his claws, I can tell you, but I was pretty nearly desperate now. So I just lay flat down on my back to let him do it.
>
> The very first tear he made was so deep that I thought it had gone right into my heart. And when he began pulling the skin off, it hurt worse than anything I've ever felt. The only thing that made me able to bear it was just the pleasure of feeling the stuff peel off.[17]

Then, with a nod to baptism, Lewis writes:

> And there was I smooth and soft as a peeled switch and smaller than I had been. Then he caught hold of me—I didn't like that much for I was very tender underneath now that I'd no skin

---

17 C. S. Lewis, *The Voyage of the Dawn Treader* (San Francisco: HarperCollins, 2005), 108–9.

on—and threw me into the water. It smarted like anything but only for a moment. After that it became perfectly delicious and as soon as I started swimming and splashing I found that all the pain had gone from my arm. And then I saw why. I'd turned into a boy again. . . .[18]

As we contemplate the glory of God reflected in the face of Christ, we are being made human again. For this is what we see—true humanity, the epitome of what is praised in Psalm 8:

what is man that you are mindful of him,
    and the son of man that you care for him?
Yet you have made him a little lower than the heavenly
        beings
    and crowned him with glory and honor.
You have given him dominion over the works of your
        hands;
    you have put all things under his feet. (Psalm 8:4–6)

It is not only that we see Jesus in his divinity, but also in his humanity. We see divine glory reflected in Christ, "beholding as in a glass" as the King James Version put it (2 Cor. 3:18 KJV). We see what the first man and woman could have been in confirmed righteousness, the divine intention for God's image bearers, and we see what we shall become by God's redeeming grace. All is not yet as it should be, in the world or in us, however,

18 Lewis, *The Voyage of the Dawn Treader*, 109.

at present, we do not yet see everything in subjection to him. But we see him who for a little while was made lower than the angels, namely Jesus, crowned with glory and honor because of the suffering of death, so that by the grace of God he might taste death for everyone. (Heb. 2:8b–9)

4. The Vale of Tears

Taking certain liberties with the homophone "vale," we can also see how seeing the glory of God in the face of Christ helps us through the travails of life. It was the face of God that sustained the psalmist through life's griefs.

> For he has not despised or abhorred
> the affliction of the afflicted,
> and he has not hidden his face from him,
> but has heard, when he cried to him. (Ps. 22:24)

Now even more so, the superiority of the new covenant is held before us in the face of Christ. The title of John Berridge's eighteenth-century hymn "Jesus, Cast a Look on Me" seeks the gaze of Christ for such comfort:

> Make me like a little child,
> Of my strength and wisdom spoiled
> Seeing only in Thy light,
> Walking only in Thy might
>
> Leaning on Thy loving breast,
> Where a weary soul can rest

Feeling well the peace of God,
Flowing from His precious blood.[19]

The removal of the veil of the old covenant, the cancellation of
our old debts, and the death sentence upon our old nature can be
personal treasures whenever we find ourselves encountering the
"vale of tears." The vale, or valley, of tears is an expression that
derives from a few very early English translations of Psalm 84:6
and has found its place in Christian literature such as Katharina
von Schlegel's hymn, "Be Still, My Soul." A line from the third
verse is: "Be still, my soul, tho' dearest friends depart; and all is
darkened in the vale of tears."[20]

Most modern translations of Psalm 84:6 have opted for "Valley
of Baca," indicating the name of a place. *Baca*, however, is Hebrew
for "weeping," and weeping does fit the context of the psalm. The
psalmist remembers with longing the beauty of God's presence
in his sanctuary in Jerusalem and the joy of worshiping in God's
presence there (84:1–2, 4). Verses 5–7 contemplate the pilgrims
who are on the way, "in whose heart are the highways to Zion"
(84:5). If weeping is the proper understanding of the translation,
it is a confident confession that even if someone is far off from
God's presence and encountering the sorrowful circumstances so
prevalent in life, that he is "blessed" if he remains mindful of what
awaits him at the end. In fact, his meditation upon the "highways
to Zion" will turn the valley of tears into "a place of springs" (84:6).

19 John Berridge, "Jesus, Cast a Look on Me," *Sion's Songs or Hymns* (London: Vallance
    and Conder, 1785), 142.
20 Katharina von Schlegel, "Be Still, My Soul," *Trinity Hymnal, rev.* (Atlanta: Great
    Commission Publications, 1997), no. 689.

Whichever way we translate the verse, the prospect of appearing (*lit.*, "be seen") before God is the psalmist's strength on the journey (84:9). Thus his appeal is for God to hear his prayer and to "look on the face of your anointed!" (84:9) because "the LORD God is a sun and shield" (84:11). However directly or indirectly the psalmist intends to draw upon the Aaronic blessing, his contemplation of God's beautiful, life-giving countenance is what preserves him through the vale of tears so that he can even call himself "blessed" (84:12)! The prospect of beholding God's face is the all-sufficient source of perseverance through the griefs of this life. When we are assailed in this world, the beatific vision of God preserves us.

> One thing have I asked of the LORD,
>   that will I seek after:
> that I may dwell in the house of the LORD
>   all the days of my life,
> to gaze upon the beauty of the LORD
> and to inquire in his temple. (Ps. 27:4)

Therefore, our cry in the vale is to call for God's face to shine upon us.

> Hear, O LORD, when I cry aloud;
>   be gracious to me and answer me!
> You have said, "Seek my face."
> My heart says to you,
>   "Your face, LORD, do I seek."
>   Hide not your face from me.
> Turn not your servant away in anger,

O you who have been my help.
Cast me not off; forsake me not,
O God of my salvation! (Ps. 27:7–9)

Beholding the glory of God in the face of Christ and knowing that we shall be like him is our comfort in and our confidence through the vale.

And the Veil of the Future

While there are four "veils/vales" removed, there is another veil through which we still look—the veil of the future. We cannot know all that we will face in this life, but what God has done in and through Jesus Christ can assure us of what the end will be and that no matter what happens between now and then, God is sovereignly directing all that will happen for our good and his glory. Knowing this removes the veil of doubt and despair that life's difficult circumstances can inflict (Rom. 8:28). The persevering power of God's glory reflected in the face of Christ also helps us when looking forward in life. Our hope in Christ lifts the veil of what the future will be like. Seeing him, who is a little lower than the angels, relativizes our present suffering. Paul wrote of his experience, "For I consider that the sufferings of this present time are not worth comparing with the glory that is to be revealed to us" (Rom. 8:18). The reflected glory of Christ's face signals our freedom from the corruption of sin, increasingly now and completely at the consummation of all things (Rom. 8:21). The Spirit that reveals to us the glory of Christ is the same Spirit that indwells us to testify to our future glorification. "The Spirit himself bears witness with our spirit that we are children of God, and if children, then heirs—heirs of God and fellow heirs with Christ, provided we suffer with him in order that we may also be glorified with him" (Rom. 8:16–17). We are indwelt by the same Spirit that raised Jesus from the dead, which means we are assured that we will be raised as well (Rom. 8:11). It is on this basis that we know nothing will separate us from God's love, which is in Christ (Rom. 8:38–39).

Practice Seeing

In the light of Christ's face these veils are lifted. Experiencing the reassuring, transformative, and hope-giving power of God's gracious gaze in Christ means we must practice seeing Christ's glory. As our King of kings, his face is our life.

> In the light of a king's face there is life,
>> and his favor is like the clouds that bring the spring rain.
>> (Prov. 16:15)

As we practice seeing his face, we will become "wise for salvation" (2 Tim. 3:15).

> Who is like the wise?
>> And who knows the interpretation of a thing?
> A man's wisdom makes his face shine,
>> and the hardness of his face is changed. (Eccles. 8:1)

How do we practice seeing our King's face? How is it exactly that we behold the light of God's glory in the face of Jesus Christ? Practically speaking, how do we avail ourselves of all the graces that are ours in God's gracious gaze realized in Christ? After all, there are times when the Bible says those who believe without seeing are blessed (John 20:29). Peter offered particular encouragement to those who love Christ without having seen him.

> Though you have not seen him, you love him. Though you do not now see him, you believe in him and rejoice with joy that is inexpressible and filled with glory, obtaining the outcome of your faith, the salvation of your souls. (1 Pet. 1:8–9)

As a young man I spent my share of time in the woods fishing, hunting, and gathering berries. Gratefully, my first ventures were with men who taught me to see, because half the challenge in the woods is knowing what to look for. I had to learn to spot the leaves and the prickly bushes before seeing the red and black raspberries, to recognize the brush cover to find the quail, to distinguish the profile of a dove or duck and recognize them against the sky, and to sense the structures around and under the water to find the fish. Even today when I do the grocery shopping, with so many choices on the shelves, I often must visualize the product I'm looking for. Like the quarry of my youth, there is a seeing that must precede finding. How is it exactly that we learn to behold Jesus Christ if we can't literally see him?

We behold the glory of God in the face of Christ with the help of the Spirit through the testimony of God's word. The Spirit, which inspired the word and now indwells us, testifies through the word of the glory of God in the face of Christ. We "see" by "hearing." Recall that at Mount Sinai, Israel did not see God. In that context, with the cloud and fire visible on the mountain,

God adamantly prohibited making any images to represent him (Deut. 4:15–31). God issued this prohibition to the people who even as he spoke were becoming impatient and forging the golden calf. Israel was not to look at an image, but to "see" God's mighty acts on their behalf as a demonstration of God's covenant, character, power, and purpose (Deut. 4:3, 34). Images of other gods abounded in the surrounding peoples, but what was unique about Israel's God was that he was a God who spoke. "Did any people ever hear the voice of a god speaking out of the midst of the fire, as you have heard, and still live?" (4:33). It was God's voice rather than his form by which they would know the Lord. "Then the LORD spoke to you out of the midst of the fire. You heard the sound of words, but saw no form; there was only a voice" (4:12). The pagan religions of the ancient world required gods who could be seen, but for ancient Israel *the ear saw more than the eye.*

This "seeing" is just as true under the new covenant. The Spirit who removes the veil is the same Spirit who inspired Scripture, which testifies to the incarnate Word, Jesus Christ. The inspired writers of Scripture told what they had seen and heard (1 John 1:1–4) so that we might hear and believe (Rom. 10:17). In addition to Scripture, Christ gave two "visible words," the sacraments of baptism and the Lord's Supper, as visible signs through which we look with the eyes of faith upon what is invisible. Yet even when we look upon these visible words (the two sacraments), we do so through what Scripture tells us about them. We are to "look not to the things that are seen but to the things that are unseen. For the things that are seen are transient, but the things that are unseen are eternal" (2 Cor. 4:18). It is through God's word that we "see" the invisible things.

Therefore, beholding the glory of God in the face of Jesus Christ becomes a matter of contemplation of who Christ is according to God's word. As Anne Steele wrote in "Thou Lovely Source of True Delight":

Thy glory o'er creation shines
But in Thy sacred Word
I read in fairer, brighter lines
My bleeding, dying Lord,
See my bleeding, dying Lord.[21]

We are meant to recount the ways in which the substance of Christ was anticipated in the Old Testament (such as in the Aaronic blessing) and appeared in the New Testament. In Christ we are blessed and kept, God's face shines upon us, and he lifts up his countenance upon us. In Christian baptism, God's name has been placed upon us. We are meant to contemplate how God in Christ has done and is doing these things. For example, stop to consider the ways God "keeps" us in Christ. Because he is our Good Shepherd, Christ has promised that no one will snatch us from his hand (John 10:12, 28–29). On the cross he cast out the ruler of this world (John 12:31). In union with Christ by faith we have been "delivered . . . from the domain of darkness and transferred . . . to the kingdom of his beloved Son" (Col. 1:13). Therefore, nothing "will be able to separate us from the love of God in Christ Jesus our Lord" (Rom. 8:39). Similarly, by faith in

---

21 Anne Steele, "Thou Lovely Source of True Delight," *The National Baptist Hymnal*, ed. R. H. Boyd and William Rosborough (Nashville, TN: National Baptist Publishing Board, 1904), 198.

Christ, God's name has been placed upon us (Rev. 3:12). Christ has given us peace (John 14:27).

Everything that was pronounced to Israel in the Aaronic blessing has been secured, is being given, and will be ours in fullness in what Christ has done, is doing by his Spirit, and will do at the consummation of the ages. Therefore, we receive the blessings of the Aaronic blessing by faith in contemplation of the person and work of Jesus Christ.

Longing for God's Look

Our contemplation of Christ depends on desire. We seek things because we want them, and we want those things because we anticipate their delights. At the end of the summer in the Hundred Acre Wood, Christopher Robin and Winnie the Pooh lazed in the shade of a tree. Christopher Robin asked Pooh what he liked doing best. Pooh responded,

> "Well, . . . what I like best?" and then he had to stop and think. Because although Eating Honey was a very good thing to do, there was a moment just before you began to eat it which was better than when you were, but he didn't know what it was called. And then he thought that being with Christopher Robin was a very good thing to do . . ."[22]

We delight in the law of the Lord because that delight comes from the Lord of the law (Psalm 1). The first generation freed from Egypt struggled to recognize this truth. Psalm 81 is a tragic

22 A. A. Milne, *The House at Pooh Corner* (London: Methuen Children's Books, 1928), 168–69.

recounting of their failure to trust God's goodness. The psalmist appeals to his reader to not repeat their mistakes:

> But he would feed you with the finest of the wheat,
>   and with honey from the rock I would satisfy you.
>   (Ps. 81:16)

Jesus Christ is our "lovely source of true delight,"[23] and contemplating his loveliness as the "dear desire of every nation [makes him the] joy of every longing heart."[24] Therefore, we must long for a look.

> One thing have I asked of the LORD,
>   that will I seek after . . .
> to gaze upon the beauty of the LORD
>   and to inquire in his temple. (Ps. 27:4)

To be looked upon by the face of God means to be loved, but it also means to be enthralled. Therefore, we unmask since Christ has been unveiled. When we see not just *what* God sees but *how* God looks upon us, we can say, "I am my beloved's and my beloved is mine" (Song 6:3). This is a far superior look compared to the selfies that populate our social media. Selfies are mediated representations of ourselves that we can retake until we present ourselves to the world exactly as we want to be seen. The smartphone camera didn't invent the selfie, but it did technologize

23 Steele, "Thou Lovely Source of True Delight."
24 Charles Wesley, "Come, Thou Long-Expected Jesus," *Trinity Hymnal*, rev. ed. (Atlanta: Great Commission Publications, 1997), no. 196.

what people have always done—make masks and veils. God in Christ sees the real us. He sees us as we really are and as we will be one day. Currently, we live in a selfie world. Consequently, we fall under the curse of Oscar Wilde's *Dorian Gray*, frozen and fossilized in a self-manufactured beauty. But as with Queen Orual, in Lewis's *Till We Have Faces*, preoccupation with self-presentation led to a loss of self. In our self-representation, we put on frozen Botox faces, preventing the wrinkles and freezing the soft tissue of our souls that complete our smiles in our eyes. When we live to be noticed by others, we void the look that God has already given us. The gaze of God liberates us from being defined by the gaze of others so that we may see ourselves in the light of God's favor.[25]

Conclusion

The last time I saw my brother John, he, our brother Tom, and I began reminiscing about songs from our high school years. John was on palliative care and in the final stages of esophageal cancer. Not able to eat or drink for several months and taking nutrition and water only through a tube, he was emaciated but talkative. He sat on the couch, where he now slept most of the day and night with his cat, Rascal, amid all the bric-a-brac and doodads he had accumulated in his public housing apartment. John's life choices had often been unkind to himself, but everyone in our

---

25 This paragraph is adapted from a chapel sermon at Reformed Theological Seminary Orlando in December 2020, which developed into an article-length treatment "We Still Have Faces" in *Reformed Faith and Practice* that same month, excerpts of which are included here by permission. Glodo, "We Still Have Faces," *Reformed Faith & Practice* 5, no. 3 (December 2020), 10–19.

small town would say he was the nicest guy in the world. When it became apparent that his time was short, I mentally labored as to how to speak about spiritual things with him. He had been raised in the church, had heard the gospel many times, and seen enough of hypocritical church people to justify his current distance from the church. It wasn't that he disbelieved, it just wasn't clear that he believed. In a past conversation a family member had had with him, he had adamantly insisted that he had no sins that needed forgiving.

Hoping to have the opportunity to talk faith with him, I had enclosed some Scripture passages that I thought might encourage him in a letter several weeks before this visit. Among them was Psalm 90, which includes, "So teach us to number our days that we may get a heart of wisdom" (90:12). Knowing that he would not reach the psalmist's allotted seventy years (90:10), it seemed a fitting passage to offer him comfort in Christ.

Having taught himself to play the guitar, John had been in rock-and-roll bands his whole life, as witnessed by the half dozen or so guitars ranging about his apartment. So it was expected that we might get around to talking about the great songs of the 1970s. Perhaps Tom or I mentioned "Dust in the Wind," a 1977 classic from the band Kansas inspired by Ecclesiastes: "I have seen everything that is done under the sun, and behold, all is vanity and a striving after wind" (Eccles. 1:14). John unexpectedly raised his head and said somewhat sharply, "I never liked that song!" Since he was especially good at the classic songs like "Stairway to Heaven" and "Hotel California," Tom and I were surprised. Tom asked, "Why not?" to which John replied, "Because people are more than just dust in the wind."

I picked up the page of the letter I had sent him and pointed to Psalm 90:3—"You return man to dust and say, 'Return, O children of man!'"—and explained what it meant to "return." In response he readily agreed, in essence, that "without faith it is impossible to please God" (Heb. 11:6). We soon ended our time by reading the whole of Psalm 90 and praying from it. Whether that moment along with being raised in the church and a lifetime of being loved by many Christians was of eternal consequence, we will one day know. But he grasped one of the most profound consequences of the beatific vision—that though we are made from the dust, we were made to be more than dust and to return to the dust.

The fullness of the Aaronic blessing realized and revealed in the incarnate glory of God in Christ makes us look at ourselves in the light of the gospel. This gospel light shines in the face of Christ by the power of the Spirit. As we behold the glory of God in the face of Jesus Christ not only is our relationship to God transformed but we are transformed. It enabled Paul to regard all his considerable agonies for the sake of the gospel as "light momentary affliction" because our trials are "preparing for us an eternal weight of glory beyond all comparison" (2 Cor. 4:17). For Christian in *Pilgrim's Progress*, the highways to Zion and a vision of Christ were in his heart to sustain him through all the difficulties of his journey to the Celestial City. When asked by Prudence about those times when Christian felt his sin most vanquished, he replied:

. . . when I think what I saw on the Cross, that will do it; and when I look upon my 'broidered Coat, that will do it; also when I look into the Roll that I carry in my bosom, that will do it; and when my thoughts wax warm about whether I am going, that will do it.[26]

This is the equipment of our earthly pilgrimage: a vision of our Savior, his righteousness with which we have been clothed by faith, the testimony of Scripture, and the hope of glory, all in the provisions of the Aaronic blessing and its fulfillment in the glory of God in the face of Jesus Christ. In the joy of life's journey lived in the light of Christ's face we can be confident by faith that "just as we have borne the image of the man of dust, we shall also bear the image of the man of heaven" (1 Cor. 15:49).

For Further Reflection

1. What would you say is the difference between reading the Bible and contemplating Christ in the Bible?

2. Heidelberg Catechism questions 1 and 2 state:

Question 1: *What is your only comfort in life and death?*

Answer: That I am not my own, but belong with body and soul, both in life and in death, to my faithful Saviour Jesus Christ. He has fully paid for all my sins with His precious blood, and has set me free from all the power of the devil. He also preserves me in such a way that without the will of my heavenly Father not a hair can fall from my head; indeed, all things must work

---

26 Bunyan, *Pilgrim's Progress*, 51.

together for my salvation. Therefore, by His Holy Spirit He also assures me of eternal life and makes me heartily willing and ready from now on to live for Him.

Question 2: *What do you need to know in order to live and die in the joy of this comfort?*

Answer: First, how great my sins and misery are; second, how I am delivered from all my sins and misery; third, how I am to be thankful to God for such deliverance.[27]

The three things in question 2 that characterize the basic rhythms of the Christian life are often summarized as "guilt-grace-gratitude." How do each of these bring you to look at yourself when seen in the light of the glory of God in the face of Jesus Christ?

---

27 Heidelberg Catechism, Questions 1–2, (Grand Rapids, MI: CRC Publications, 1989), 9–12.

5

The Aaronic Blessing and Others

The Consequences of the Blessing
Part 2—Seeing Others Face-to-Face

ON A SATURDAY MORNING in November 2020, my wife received word that her eighty-nine-year-old father had been taken to the hospital due to a stroke. It became clear very quickly to the medical personnel that there would be no meaningful recovery. This marked the start of a wearying eight-day vigil waiting for the inevitable. He had been a hardy farmer his whole adult life, always in motion—even on the day before his stroke he had been operating a backhoe to do pre-winter maintenance on a pond dam. Given his strength and vitality, he didn't relinquish earthly life easily. Providentially, my wife and I had just reread for perhaps the fifth time Wendell Berry's account of the death of Burley Coulter in which "the membership" (Burley's relatives and friends from Port William) conspire against the medical-industrial complex to give Burley the dignified and loving death he was due.[1] Additionally we had recently read Lydia Dugdale's *The Lost Art of Dying: Reviving Forgotten Wisdom.*[2]

Dugdale, as a physician and ethicist, traces the development of the *ars moriendi*, the "art of dying," within the Christian tradition and the loss of its wisdom and practices caused by the medicalization of death and other social influences. Her overall case is that to die well, we must live well by preparing to die and participating in death with others. Death should be a community matter, not simply an individual matter. To live well in order to die well, we must participate as families, friends, and in the case of Christians, churches. With these thoughts fresh on her mind, my wife instinctively and organically began keeping an organized vigil with her father along with her siblings, mother, and my family. Although my father-in-law showed no signs of recognition or awareness, we read Scripture, prayed, sang hymns, or else simply sat at his bedside for the next eight days. The hospital, closed for regular care due to the pandemic, was sacrosanctly quiet. The vigil had a genuinely holy nature to it.

During one of my watches, I took particular note of his hands. He wasn't a tall man, but his hands were big for his size, rough and strong from seven decades of farming. I began to recall the hands of all my departed family. Aged hands are beautiful, and for those who have labored hard with their hands, their hands can contain as much life as their faces. But

---

1 Wendell Berry, "Fidelity," *That Distant Land: The Collected Stories* (Berkeley: Counterpoint Press, 2004), 372–427.

2 Lydia Dugdale, *The Lost Art of Dying: Reviving Forgotten Wisdom* (San Francisco: HarperOne, 2020).

during another one of those vigils by myself, I felt a blush as I realized I had not been looking at his face. I'm sure this was partially due to how his face appeared. His eyes were hollow and closed, his mouth slightly drawn, but for the most part my averted gaze wasn't because he was hard to look at. It was because, I imagined, it would be hard for him to be seen like that. While some people only want to be seen at their best, most people don't want to be seen at their worst. When we see someone in a circumstance where they might be embarrassed, we avert our eyes out of respect for them. It's a form of kindness. That's why I wasn't looking at my father-in-law's face. Here is what I realized: by not looking him in the face, not looking at his closed eyes, I was actually withholding dignity from him. All that he had been and lived had not left him even though his bodily strength was nearly spent. All that he had said and seen in his fourscore and ten years was not unsaid or unseen because his mouth and his eyes could no longer speak and see. Most importantly, the image in which he had been created, the image of the Creator, had not departed. I realized, to give him honor and dignity, I must look at his face. While his strength, sight, and speech were gone (who knew whether he heard us?), the image of God had not dimmed.

What does this event in my life have to do with the Aaronic blessing? The Aaronic blessing as climactically realized in Christ not only transforms how we look at ourselves, it transforms how we look at others. The gospel is a reminder and renewal of our vision to see the image of God not just in ourselves but in others. There are four major implications to God's gracious gaze as it points us to see God's image in others.

1. Looking at Others

The first implication is that we see others. We are reminded that being designed for dignity means being designed for community. Looking at others with value begins in the beginning with the creation of people. As we learned earlier, when God made Adam in his image and likeness, the term "likeness" connoted a three-dimensional object. God made us with bodies not just souls. We have eyes on our faces and limited peripheral vision, limbs with limited range, ears that point forward, and other limitations that require us to depend on others. Our knowledge of the world, and more importantly, even our knowledge of ourselves, cannot be full without others. We will never see the backs of our heads or our elbows in an unmediated way. We will never see our facial expressions and hear our tone of voice as others see and hear them. God made human beings as social creatures. It is in the design of our nature. We are social beings not simply in the sense that we need social contact or that other people keep us from being lonely. There is always the person who might insist that they don't need and prefer not to depend on others. It is deeper than that. To be isolated is contrary to nature, contrary to the nature of how God made human beings. When God had created Adam, he said, "It is not good that the man should be alone" (Gen. 2:18). So he made Eve out of Adam. The remedy to the "not good" was not only for the social bond of marriage but also for the completion of the work of creation, which would have been incomplete with one human but was complete with two. To be in the image of God means to be an inherently social creature whose fullness and purpose as a creature is incomplete without interpersonal relationships.

Pablo Picasso's portraits are unmistakable. In his Synthetic Cubism style, he painted parts of the face in seemingly random positions, like a poorly executed version of Mr. Potato Head. Interestingly, Picasso first began to paint portraits partly because he had prosopagnosia or "face blindness." Face blindness is not a problem with the eye but rather a neurological problem that can be congenital or the result of injury. Occurring with varying degrees of severity, a person with face blindness has difficulty recognizing others visually. Close friends, relatives, and even oneself may be unrecognizable. In his portraits Picasso broke down the face into its components, like the pieces of a puzzle, and then tried to represent them in two dimensions. The striking novelty of his portraits is largely due to his attempt to represent in two dimensions what actually exists in three dimensions. Human beings, beings in the "likeness" of God, are bodily beings who cannot be fully known without knowledge by and from others.

Think of it this way: if God endowed a creature to reflect his image, yet there was no other creature to recognize and revel in the glory of that image, God would receive no honor or glory through that image-bearing creature. An artist creates so that others might see. God created image bearers in order that they might not only reflect his image but also recognize his image in others. This is why the fall was so disruptive to the social realm. The wreckage of the image in us, our refusal to recognize it in others, and the way we see ourselves as existing for ourselves is exhibit A for the fall of humanity.

2. Looking at Others Differently

The second implication of God's gracious gaze as it points us toward others is that we look at others differently. To look at God

THE AARONIC BLESSING AND OTHERS

fully in and through Christ clearly has implications for our worship of God and our relationship to God. However, right worship of God has its corollary in recognizing and revering the image of God in others. To see the glory of God in the face of Jesus Christ means we look at others differently.

Cain's fratricide was rooted in disparity of worship. Neighbor love and God love are inseparable like two sides of the same coin. It is a contradiction to love God and not love neighbor and vice versa. To truly love another inherently involves loving the other. A subtle but powerful expression of this is found in Psalm 115. After the opening appeal for God's glory in the first verse, the psalmist asks:

> Why should the nations say
>   "Where is their God?"
> Our God is in the heavens;
>   he does all that he pleases. (115:2–3)

A polemic follows, mocking the gods of the other nations, naming seven body parts of their inert gods that can't perform the functions they represent. Their mouths can't speak oracles, their eyes can't see into the future, their ears can't hear petitions, their noses can't smell offerings, their hands can't save, their feet can't carry, and their throats can't grunt or groan to express emotions. These are things even animals can do. Even though the gods of the nations are gilded, they are gelded, impotent because they are dead gods. Because people become like the gods they worship, idol worshipers will become impotent and dead (115:8). From there, the psalm goes on to express trust and confidence in the

God of Israel, who remembers, blesses, and prospers his people because he is a living God.

Two things in particular are relevant here. First of all, why would the other nations say, "Where is their God?" (115:2). It is because unlike the other nations, Israel's sanctuary did not contain an image of their God. Does this mean Israel had no image of their God? Absolutely not! Every Israelite was an image of God, living images, as the opening chapters of Genesis say. Just as the early Christians were called "atheists," Old Testament Israel, according to the psalmist, is mocked for idol-less worship. The psalmist is nonplussed by this criticism because Israel's God was in the heavens, the heavens that belonged to him (115:16). From there God rules the earth and does whatever he pleases (115:3). What does it please Israel's God to do? This is the second noteworthy thing for us to recognize. It pleases God to give the earth "to the children of man" (115:16). Israel enjoyed the bounty of the earth as a gift from their covenant Lord. It also pleases Israel's God to bless all Israel, from the house of the high priest Aaron to the very least among them and even to non-Israelite God-fearers who become worshipers of him (115:12–13). The merism of "the small and the great" indicates God's indiscriminate care for all his people. The law of Moses, in its particular concerns for the widow, the orphan, and the stranger, systemize the concern for equity that is based on the fundamental notion that all are image bearers of God. Israel didn't need an image of God in the sanctuary because every worshiper of God was God's image.

This concept leads us back to the point that love for God and love for neighbor are not two things but two sides of the same coin. Faithful keeping of the law meant not only right love for

God in worship but also right love for God by loving neighbor. This is clear from examples such as the diatribe of Isaiah toward professed Sabbath keepers (Isaiah 58). Those who cry out to God in protestation that they have humbly sought the Lord through fasting (58:1–5) must scrutinize their religious devotion in light of the Sabbath's obligations for justice and mercy (58:6–10). Genuine fasting frees the oppressed (58:6) and feeds the hungry (58:7), and true sabbath keeping is compassion for the lowly rather than seeking one's pleasure (58:13–14). James reflects this same understanding of the relationship between love of God and love of neighbor in his polemic against the unbridled tongue. "No human being can tame the tongue. It is a restless evil, full of deadly poison. With it we bless our Lord and Father, and with it we curse people who are made in the likeness of God" (James 3:8–9). James exposes the fundamental contradiction between treating God and neighbor differently.

In the ancient world as well as in many places today, no one gets by with dishonoring an image of the king. In the book of Daniel, three Hebrew princes were thrown into the furnace for their refusal to honor Nebuchadnezzar's golden image. Rather than bow to the emperor's image, they prayed, "Now therefore, O our God, listen to the prayer of your servant and to his pleas for mercy, and for your own sake, O Lord, make your face to shine upon your sanctuary, which is desolate" (Dan. 9:17). Even in contemporary times, people take a great risk when failing to honor the image of an autocrat. The toppling of statues from Lenin and Stalin to Saddam Hussein confirm the connection between respect for the person and treatment of the person's image. On the other hand, honoring the image of a king honors that king. While the other nations bowed before the speechless, deaf, non-ambulatory, and otherwise impotent images of their gods, Israel was to honor King Yahweh by loving their neighbors, his living images.

3. Looking at Different Others

There is a third implication for God's gracious gaze in Christ. It causes us to look at different others. By "different others" I mean we take notice of those individuals we might otherwise overlook or look down upon. In the light of Christ's face we must see such people as bearers of the same image we behold in the face of Christ. David Grossman's controversial 1995 book *On Killing* drew upon studies from World War II that concluded most combat soldiers didn't fire their weapons in combat, and even when they did they often didn't actually aim at their enemies.[3] The reason, the studies concluded, was that people have an innate resistance to killing other human beings, especially when those other human beings resemble themselves. Based on the study's findings, infantry training was dramatically modified through behavioral conditioning in order to overcome that natural resistance. Consequently, the fire rate and kill rate climbed dramatically to 50 percent in the Korean War and 90 percent in Vietnam. Tragically, there occurred incidents of indiscriminate killing such as the infamous Mỹ Lai massacre. There were also the hidden wounds of the many veterans who experienced post-combat stress and sometimes long-lasting psychological difficulties. While Grossman's application of these developments to contemporary problems of murder and violence

---

3   David Grossman, *On Killing: The Psychological Cost of Learning to Kill in War and Society* (Boston: Little, Brown, and Co., 1995).

was debated, the larger point about how human views human is relevant to how we look at others.

It is entirely possible to look at other human beings, even at fellow believers in Christ, and not see the image of God. Recognition of God's image is vital for fostering neighbor love. This is actually more to the point of Jesus's well-known parable of the good Samaritan than the charitable acts that the Samaritan performed (Luke 10:25–37). The parable is rightly interpreted as commending compassion toward someone in need and condemning a certain religiosity that ignores such needs. Let there be no mistaking how great the contrast was between the two described sets of behaviors toward the beaten man. Just count the verbs. The priest and Levite "passed by"—a minimal description—but the Samaritan "came," "had compassion," "bound up," "brought," "took care," "took" and "gave" money to the innkeeper, said "take care," and promised to "repay." Yet as striking as was the contrast between the religious professionals (a Levite and priest) and an unclean heretic (the Samaritan), there is a deeper, more poignant, and more subversive point Jesus is making in the story. The lawyer's (i.e., scribe's) question, which prompted this parable, is the key.

At first the lawyer asks, "Teacher, what shall I do to inherit eternal life?" (10:25). For readers today that question sounds like part of an evangelistic exchange in which the outcome is a personal, individual saving faith that assures the asker they will go to heaven when they die. In its historical context, however, this is not what the question asked. The lawyer's question would have been understood by those listening as asking something more than reaching heaven. To "inherit life," understood against the background of the promises to Abraham and Israel, would mean something like, "How can I be assured that I have a share in the inheritance of the people of God?" Whatever his motive, he wanted to know Jesus's answer to "Who really belongs to the people of God?" When Jesus responded with the two great commands to love God and neighbor, the lawyer pressed the question in order "to justify himself" (10:29). He is not asking the question with the concept of imputed forensic righteousness as the basis of justification. The lawyer's question is not unrelated to justification, but his specifying question makes his intent clearer. "And who is my neighbor?" (10:29). It is in response to this question that Jesus told this parable of the good Samaritan.

In the parable, the two religious professionals would be rendered unclean by assisting the wounded man and are compelled to pass by him in order to continue rendering their official religious functions. They see standing with God as an individual matter between God and themselves, and aiding the beaten man would be a disruption to their standing with God. The person who turns out to be the good neighbor is the Samaritan, who is regarded as unclean from birth, heretical in beliefs, and a sworn enemy of Jews. He doesn't just do the actions of a good neighbor, but in doing them proves himself to be a true neighbor, a part of the community of those who belong to God's kingdom. That is, his actions demonstrate that he is a true citizen of the community that will share in God's inheritance. So the most subversive aspect of Jesus's answer wasn't that the beaten man was a neighbor to someone in need, but that according to the law of Moses the Samaritan was a true neighbor to the lawyer and the Israelites. The implication for the lawyer wasn't "love your neighbor like the Samaritan did," but "love the Samaritan who is your neighbor and a fellow heir of the kingdom of God!" The lawyer had to look at the Samaritan as a legitimate image bearer of God rather than through his own ethno-racial-religio-national lenses.

In our modern day, Senator Ben Sasse of Nebraska has attempted to reconcile our unprecedented prosperity with our equally unprecedented anxiety and rancor in his book, *Them: Why We Hate Each Other—and How to Heal*.[4] He argues that the root of societal vitriol isn't ultimately political. Yes, there are real differences about very important things in the political arena today, but that has always been true of political and governmental systems. What's different today is the extremes that normal people are now willing to go to dehumanize one another. Sasse believes these trends come from a loss of a sense of place and a decline in human-to-human relationships. One significant source of this dehumanization is the uncritical adoption and use of technology.

If we are going to rebuild community in the digital age—if we are going to be happy—we are going to need to realize anew that humans shouldn't aim to be "free from" real people and real places, but aim rather to be "free to" grow roots into those people and places.[5]

Additionally, when most of our goods and services are obtained from impersonal sources in unknown locations rather than a corner store, it is much easier for the quality to lag and the dissatisfaction to ramp up. In my youth I worked at a local grocery

---

4 Ben Sasse, *Them: Why We Hate Each Other—and How to Heal* (New York: St. Martin's, 2018).

5 Sasse, *Them*, 168.

store one summer. The mayor was a co-owner of this grocery store. So in addition to his government role, he delivered groceries when asked. (And fun fact, he delivered these groceries by placing the boxed order *on*—not in!—the trunk of his car since speeds that would have lost the boxes were unnecessary in our small town.) If anyone had the misfortune of a house fire, the local restaurant owner, dry cleaner, and baker were among those who arrived on the fire truck. It would have been difficult for anyone to post a scorching Yelp review about our local hardware store when one had to sit next to the owner in the church choir the following Sunday.

Our cultural conundrum is enormously complex, and the solution will take more than a simplistic return to Andy Griffith's *Mayberry*, a reality Sasse readily acknowledges in his book. But it is clear that the gospel calls us back to a rehumanized view of human nature in general and of individuals in particular. After all, it is while we were yet enemies of God that Christ died for us (Rom. 5:8). Rehumanizing the image of God is essential to sustaining love for neighbor and especially for loving enemies, praying for persecutors, blessing those who curse us, and suffering for doing good (Matt. 5:44; Rom. 12:14; 1 Pet. 3:13–17).

Recently, emotional intelligence (EQ) has emerged as a greater predictor of success than sheer intellect (IQ). Since identification of the EQ concept in the 1950s and emergence of the term in the 1960s, EQ has become a veritable growth industry as well as a buzzword often without clear meaning. Rather than being a single quality, EQ is really a combination of qualities, with empathy being one of the most vital qualities. Empathy is different from sympathy. Sympathy feels *for* a person while empathy feels *as if* we were that person. We can find it difficult to empathize with someone because we haven't had their experiences and can't look at things exactly the way they do. Sometimes we might even be wary about empathy because it might cause us to doubt our personal convictions. We might worry that if we begin to appreciate the difficulties or challenges particular people face in living up to God's standards we will be tempted to lower biblical standards. In the incarnation, God didn't simply feel for us but entered into humanity to demonstrate that he identifies with us. Empathy is not the problem, but rather the will to love others as God loves them. Empathy harnessed by the gospel is a powerful motivator and enabler of bringing gospel change.[6] Jesus, in his human nature, was moved by empathy to have compassion on people when he "saw" them (Matt. 9:36; 14:14; Mark 6:34; Luke 7:13).

Seeing every person's humanity reflected in the new man Jesus Christ should cause us to take notice of those whom we naturally would overlook. This is the very point made by Jesus in his last public teaching in Matthew's Gospel. On the day of final judgment there will be a great separation between those who truly belong to Christ and those who do not (Matt. 25:31–46). The separation will be based on whether people fed, gave drink, welcomed, clothed, and visited Jesus when he was in need. Both sheep and goats are surprised and ask when they did or didn't do these things (25:37–40, 44). Jesus answered that it was when they did or didn't do these things for "the least of these" (25:40,

---

6 Ken Sande, author of *The Peacemaker* (Grand Rapids, MI: Baker, 2004), has integrated gospel-centered peacemaking protocols with insights from emotional intelligence so that people can experience true shalom in his Relational Wisdom 360 protocols (www .RW360.com).

45). The operative verb in both inquiries is "see" (25:39, 44). "When did we *see* you?" Unbeknownst to both the righteous and the unrighteous at the time, when they looked upon the "least of these" it was as though they were looking upon Jesus himself.

The needs of those Jesus mentions are informative for us as well. The needs of the hungry and thirsty are observable. The stranger is recognizable for not being familiar. The exposure of the naked is blatantly observable, but in a way that can cause people to instinctively look away. The sick and the prisoner are often out of sight, and therefore easily out of mind. But the righteous "see" them all and respond. Those on Christ's left, the goats, didn't see the "least of these," and in the final judgment they become those who "will go away into eternal punishment" (25:46).

The title that Jesus gives himself in this passage further reinforces the point about "seeing different others." Matthew's Gospel uses the word "king" almost twice as much as Mark and Luke and a third again as much as John. Matthew begins his Gospel referring to David, "the king" (Matt. 1:6). In highly ironic usage in the story of the wise men, Herod is thrice called "the king" even though as an Idumean (Edomite) he doesn't have a legitimate claim to Israel's throne. The wise men whom he interrogates tell Herod they are looking for the "king of the Jews" (Matt. 2:2). Several times throughout Matthew's Gospel, Jesus refers to kings and their ways in order to teach his disciples about the kingdom of heaven (Matt. 17:25; 18:23; 22:1–14), one of Matthew's principal themes. Only later, when being tried before Pilate, does Jesus concede that he is "King of the Jews" (Matt. 27:11) after which he is mocked (27:29, 37, 42). In general, *others* call Jesus "King," whether in sincerity or sarcasm, not Jesus himself. Here, though, in the well-known "least of these" passage, Jesus uncharacteristically and unprecedentedly confers upon himself the title "king" (Matt. 25:34, 40). In that great day of separation between sheep and goats, he will reign with supreme authority. So he warns people in the present to see the least of these as surrogates for himself, the King. To say it in terms more clearly connected to the Aaronic blessing, Christ desires for us to see his glorious image in the most needy people we meet. The glory of God in the face of Christ should restore our vision to see Christ's image in them. By revering God's image in the least of these, we become more like the one we worship.

4. The Body Has a Face

The final way the glory of God in the face of Christ should cause us to look at others is to see the bodies to which these faces belong. What we've learned about the social dimension of God's image in creation and now in redemption leads us to recognize that every follower of Christ needs and is needed by Christ's body. In 1 Corinthians 12, Paul expounded the metaphor of a body in order to instruct the members of the church in Corinth about the nature of their relationships to one another. Having lived formerly under the directives of the mute idols of the pagan temples, they have now professed Christ as Lord and should live by his words (12:1–3). Earlier Paul had appealed to the oneness of Christ himself to address factionalism within the church (1:13). So as we read 1 Corinthians 12, he now applies Christ's oneness to operative relationships within the church. Believers are united to one Christ by one Spirit who is one with the Father and the Son (12:4–11). The unity of the Triune God as the basis of their unity with one another has implications for how they are to relate to one another in the use of the gifts given them by the Spirit (12:12–20). The social order this produces should reflect the subversive order intruded upon the world by Christ's ignominious death on the cross. In other words, the scandal and folly of the cross (1:21–23) is to manifest itself in a scandalous (according to the world's opinions) social order among those who believe. This Christian social order makes the weaker members of the body indispensable and the less honorable people those who receive greater honor (12:22–24).

While Paul doesn't explicitly say that Christ is the head in 1 Corinthians 12, he is clearly working out the implications that Jesus is (see Eph. 1:22; 4:15; 5:23; Col. 1:18; 2:19). Just as with the metaphor of God's face, we must not slide past the implications of the body metaphor. Although Christ has a physical resurrected body as he sits at the right hand of God, the church is also his body. The church is his body in a different, though real, sense. The church on earth is the body of the living Christ on earth.

We must also be clear about what this does not mean. The Son of God is still the Son without the incarnation. Jesus Christ is still the Son incarnate without the church. Christ and the church are the body in different senses, but the church as Christ's body with him as head is the whole Christ on earth. This idea can be misunderstood and misapplied, such as in the Roman Catholic understanding that it exclusively constitutes the body of Christ on earth. Properly understood and applied, however, Paul's metaphor of the body says that the way Christ offers himself on earth is through his church. If we want to come to Christ, we must come to his church. If we wish to be united to him in his death through baptism, eat and drink with him at his table, experience fellowship with him, hear him speak through his word, and see God's glory reflected in his face, we must come to his church. This is often a novel concept to many evangelical Protestant Christians, though it was believed and taught by the sixteenth-century Reformers who reclaimed the so-called "doctrines of grace" and the *"solas"* of the Reformation. The cult of individualism fostered by the Enlightenment is virile, particularly in Western society. The necessity of the church for salvation must be carefully nuanced.[7] Yet we must not let that nuancing obscure the glory of what the body metaphor exhibits. The body of Christ (the church) is the means by which Christ offers himself that we may behold the glory of God in his face.

In Flannery O'Connor's "Parker's Back" story, the wayward O. E. (Obadiah Elihu) Parker is unhappily married to the hellfire preaching Sarah Ruth. Sarah Ruth is particularly disdainful and judgmental of the tattoos that cover O. E. everywhere except his back. One day while plowing, O. E. was blinded by the white-hot sun and carelessly slammed the farm owner's tractor into the lone tree standing at the crest of the domed field. The collision threw him onto his back, and the lone tree and his cast-off shoes burst into flame. He was terrified by the theophanic vision of the burning tree and shoes and determined to settle his torment and placate his wife by having a Byzantine Christ tattooed over the entirety of his back. After the first of what would take two full days, the tattoo artist showed Parker the progress of the work. Expecting to see the complete face of Jesus on his back, Parker saw

---

7 For more, see Michael J. Glodo, *"Sola Ecclesia*: The Lost Reformation Doctrine," *New Horizons*, May 2001: 4–5, 6.

THE CONSEQUENCES OF THE BLESSING, PART 2

a mouth, the beginning of heavy eyebrows, a straight nose, but the face was empty; the eyes had not yet been put in . . . "It don't have eyes," Parker cried out. "That'll come," the artist said, "in due time. We have another day to go yet."[8]

In a manner of speaking, the face of Christ has been filled in with the body of Christ. Having beheld the glory of God in the face of Christ, Christians can look at other people as image bearers of that same glory, especially recognizing those who are most easily overlooked, and Christians can look to the body of Christ for the regular appearing of that glory in Christ. Christians must look particularly to those members of the bonded, covenanted body of Christ to whom they have been united by their living head, Jesus Christ.

A Greater Righteousness

Pastor and theologian Dietrich Bonhoeffer lived, ministered, wrote, and died in a context when his nation's nationalist aspirations bore fruit in unimaginable atrocities. Between World War I and World War II the place of the church in German public life was tenuous. In order to maintain its place within the culture, the broader German church often accommodated political developments. With church support high for the Nationalist Socialist Party, especially among Protestants, the dissenting Confessing Church movement emerged to distance itself from a nationalistic syncretism of the Christian faith. Bonhoeffer was prominent among these dissenters. In his classic book *The Cost of Discipleship*

8   Flannery O'Connor, "Parker's Back," *Everything That Rises Must Converge*, in *Collected Works*, Library of America (New York: Library of America, 1988), 668.

a reflection on the Sermon on the Mount, Bonhoeffer wrestled with the enigma of how a person can believe themselves to be in right standing with God while being blind to the plight of others. He identifies the root of the problem as "cheap grace."

> Cheap grace is preaching forgiveness without repentance; it is baptism without the discipline of community; it is the Lord's Supper without confession of sin; it is absolution without personal confession. Cheap grace is grace without discipleship, grace without the cross, grace without the living, incarnate Jesus Christ.[9]

Alternatively, the grace of the gospel "is costly, because it is a call to discipleship; . . . It is costly, because it costs people their lives, it is grace, because it thereby makes them live."[10] Bonhoeffer believed that a chief fallacy leading to cheap grace is seeing discipleship as strictly an individual matter. Cheap grace reduces the moral demands of discipleship, particularly one's obligations toward others. This, he believes, is fatal to discipleship because it tames discipleship into mere citizenship. Bonhoeffer saw the Sermon on the Mount as exposing such an individualistic and erroneous understanding of righteousness limited only to one's standing before God. He expresses this in his comment on Jesus's declaration, "For I tell you, unless your righteousness exceeds that of the scribes and Pharisees, you will never enter the kingdom of heaven" (Matt. 5:20). Bonhoeffer comments on the Greek

9   Dietrich Bonhoeffer, *Discipleship*, in *Dietrich Bonhoeffer Works* (Minneapolis: Fortress, 2003), 4:44.
10 Bonhoeffer, *Discipleship*, 45.

perisson, translated "exceeds," in relation to the terms for "the self," *to auto*.

> The περισσόν never dissolves into το αύτο. It is the great mistake of a false Protestant ethic to assume that loving Christ can be the same as loving one's native country, or friendship, or profession, that the better righteousness and *justitia civilis* [civil justice] are the same.[11]

What Bonhoeffer is saying is that the "exceeding" or "better" righteousness Jesus commended is one that cannot be attained solely as an individual. "The community of Jesus' disciples, the community of better righteousness, is the visible community, that took the step beyond the orders of the world."[12]

The righteousness of the kingdom of heaven, a righteousness that is greater than the righteousness of the scribes and the Pharisees, must be sought in the society of other disciples. This is seen in the very nature of Jesus's commands in the Sermon on the Mount. His teaching about anger, reconciliation, lust, divorce, oaths, retaliation, neighbor love, enemy love, and generosity are impossible and irrelevant if he were only describing our individual standing before God (Matt. 5:21–6:4). The righteousness of the kingdom of heaven must be sought in the community that is the kingdom.

Someone might ask, "But isn't the righteousness of God a gift of his free grace?" Yes. By grace alone through faith alone in the righteousness of Christ alone we are justified before God in the legal, Pauline sense (Rom. 4–5; Eph. 2:1–10). Christ's obedience

---

11 Bonhoeffer, *Discipleship*, 144.
12 Bonhoeffer, *Discipleship*, 145.

is the basis of our justification before God (Rom. 4:24–25). Those of us who stand in the tradition of the Protestant Reformation rightly stress that our salvation is based on God's grace and not the merits of our good works, for it is by faith alone we are justified before God (Eph. 2:8). But a narrow or exclusive emphasis on individual justification severs a part of Christ and his work from his whole person and work.[13]

It's no less possible in our day than in Bonhoeffer's for a person to claim to be in right standing with God and be oblivious or even dehumanizing toward fellow image bearers. During his time on earth, Jesus regularly humanized people on the margins so that we would learn to not overlook them. We must look where Jesus looked, and in doing so, we are to recognize they share the *imago Dei*, however obscured by the ravages of sin. In Bonhoeffer's day an individualistic understanding of discipleship produced a civil religion that was neither civil nor true religion (James 1:27), and we risk the same if we don't see others differently, as well as "different others."

This is what New Testament theologian John Barclay describes when the Christian community neglects the scandal of the cross as its formative principle in exchange for a certain social acceptability.

A Christ-crucified spoken to and for the elite, neatly corresponding with the standards of value that undergird the social status quo, is a vacuous gospel, all words and no substance,

---

13 While beginning with the historical "Marrow controversy," which may seem obscure to some readers, this is the larger point made in Sinclair B. Ferguson, *The Whole Christ: Legalism, Antinomianism, and Gospel Assurance—Why the Marrow Controversy Still Matters* (Wheaton, IL: Crossway, 2016).

... Without practice, experience, and social embodiment, the Christian message has no significant meaning, and is constantly in danger of canceling itself.[14]

Conclusion

The way God looks upon us in the Son is both the premise and the pattern for how we should love others. We do not, as in the words of John Gillespie McGee's "High Flight" poem, "slip the surly bonds of earth and touch the face of God."[15] Rather, we touch the face of God in acts of love toward his image. Jesus said nothing less in the parable of the returning king who commended acts of mercy done toward him as they were done to his surrogates in need. The king's subjects asked when they had done these things. The king answered, "Truly, I say to you, as you did it to one of the least of these my brothers, you did it to me" (Matt. 25:40).[16]

Beholding the gracious gaze of God in the Aaronic blessing as we behold the glory of God in the face of Christ gives us a vision of God's glory, but it also reminds us that Christ came to renew the image of God in us and others. While this vision

14 John M. G. Barclay, "Crucifixion as Wisdom: Exploring the Ideology of a Disreputable Social Movement," in *The Wisdom and Foolishness of God: First Corinthians 1–2 in Theological Exploration*, eds. Christophe Chalamet and Hans-Christoph Askani (Minneapolis: Fortress, 2015), 18.

15 John Gillespie McGee Jr. "High Flight," Poetry Foundation, December 13, 2022, https://www.poetryfoundation.org.

16 This paragraph is adapted from a chapel sermon at Reformed Theological Seminary Orlando in December 2020, which developed into an article-length treatment 'We Still Have Faces' in *Reformed Faith and Practice* that same month, excerpts of which are included here by permission. Glodo, "We Still Have Faces," *Reformed Faith & Practice* 5, no. 3 (December 2020), 10–19.

is the basis for our own transformation so that one day we will be like Christ, the glory of God in the face of Christ directs our gaze toward other image bearers, including and especially those we might not see otherwise. A home remodeler or a car restorer can look upon a run-down house or car and see the possibilities because their imaginations allow them to see what could be. Similarly, when we look upon the perfection of God's image in Christ, we are to see the possibilities of what God's grace can do and is doing among us. This is what C. S. Lewis invites us to do in his oft-cited description of what people were made to be and what they can and will be by God's grace one day:

> It may be possible for each to think too much of his own potential glory hereafter; it is hardly possible for him to think too often or too deeply about that of his neighbour. The load, or weight, or burden of my neighbour's glory should be laid on my back, a load so heavy that only humility can carry it, and the backs of the proud will be broken. It is a serious thing to live in a society of possible gods and goddesses, to remember that the dullest and most uninteresting person you can talk to may one day be a creature which, if you saw it now, you would be strongly tempted to worship, or else a horror and a corruption such as you now meet, if at all, only in a nightmare.
>
> There are no ordinary people. You have never talked to a mere mortal. Nations, cultures, arts, civilizations—these are mortal, and their life is to ours as the life of a gnat. But it is immortals whom we joke with, work with, marry, snub and exploit—immortal horrors or everlasting splendours. . . . Next

to the Blessed Sacrament itself, your neighbour is the holiest object presented to your senses.[17]

For Further Reflection

1. What are the types of people you find most difficult to love? What are the types of people you regularly pass by and don't see? Are there people who you tend to treat as nonpersons, or worse, objectify, in order to satisfy yourself? How can beholding the glory of God in Christ humanize these people in your heart and mind?

2. Considering your own social, educational, political, etc., preferred affiliations, who are the people most difficult to love that you pass by and treat as nonpersons? Do you find yourself dissonant with or conflicted about your "tribe's" attitude toward these kinds of people?

3. Take time in prayer to pray for a different or better vision to look at others differently and at "different others."

17 C. S. Lewis, *The Weight of Glory* (San Francisco: HarperOne, 2001), 45–46.

6

The Aaronic Blessing and Worship

Participation and Pastoral Practice

MY WIFE AND I WERE ONCE INVITED to "Bembe Teo," a local elite chef's term for a small gathering at his home where guests would experience some of his recent culinary creations. A *bembe* is a religious gathering or festival, and *Teo* is Spanish for "God." It was the host's desire for it to be a time of lively enjoyment and conversation around the subject of God. The evening would feature a five-course meal with each of the five courses from a different locale in his native Puerto Rico. Prior to the evening we received a menu detailing the courses, their process of preparation, what to expect from their textures and flavors, and the wine pairings being provided by a local sommelier. The meal was free. Though the chef had been a cooking show host, there would be no cameras. The purpose of the advance menu was to entice our appetites and explain the dishes so that our enjoyment would be maximized. Familiarizing us with the menu before we came allowed us simply to be free to feast and fellowship together.

In this chapter we will look at the advance menu of some aspects of worship in order to enjoy God's gracious hospitality fully. After all, worship is to be a feast where we "taste and see that the LORD is good!" (Ps. 34:8). David's invitation is specifically in the context of gathered worship. "Oh, magnify the LORD with me, and let us exalt his name together" (34:3). Worship is to be a fellowship, a gathering together in order to strengthen our bonds with one another and to encourage one another as we address "one another in psalms and hymns and spiritual songs, singing and making melody to the Lord with your heart" (Eph 5:19). Specifically, we will consider how the Aaronic blessing and the light of the glory of God in the face of Jesus Christ can enhance our feasting and fellowship when we come together for worship. Looking first at worship through the lens of the Aaronic blessing and then looking specifically at the role of benedictions can enable us to share in the "forever-pleasures" and the "fullness of joy" found at God's right hand (Ps. 16:11).

Setting the Table for Worship

The subject of worship gets a lot of attention, and opinions are not scarce. The term "worship wars" reflects the frequent intensity of these discussions. Like a powerful magnet, the subject of music often attracts the conversation away from the larger picture. Two frequent subtopics are intelligibility and accessibility. *Intelligibility* refers to how easy or difficult it is for a person (particularly the uninitiated) to understand what is going on in a worship service. *Accessibility* is related to intelligibility but has to do with the ease of participation. Because our whole study in this book began with an observation about the place of the Aaronic blessing in the context of worship, how can the Aaronic blessing cast light on our broader understanding of worship—to aid us in making worship appropriately intelligible and accessible to both Christians and visitors? We want to consider that question without falling down the "rabbit hole" of worship's complexities, yet we need to have at least a basic orientation to the dynamics of worship before we can truly answer that question.

My fifth-grade teacher, Mrs. Ross, once assigned a current event report. My subject was the Paris Peace Talks. Representatives of all parties involved in the conflict in Vietnam had gathered in Paris to try to bring an end to the hostilities. What I vividly recall from that current events assignment is that while the war raged on, the parties took ten weeks to agree on the shape of the table around which they would meet to attempt to negotiate peace. We should be clear on the basic shape of the "table" of worship to make our reflection on the Aaronic blessing helpful.

The most basic shape of worship is that God is the audience and his people the performers. This performance, though, doesn't take place in a high school gymnasium, local theater, concert venue, or sports arena. It takes place in a throne room. In every worship scene in Scripture, whether in the physical structures of the tabernacle and temple or the visionary scenes of Isaiah 6 and Revelation 4–5, the living creatures' attention is centered upon God enthroned in their midst. These prefigurations and visions of worship can shape our worship on earth. It is God's actions and attributes that are the subject of praise and thanksgiving, his mercy pled in confession, and his help that is sought in petitions.

God speaks in the context of worship through the preaching of his word, in the Scripture we read (many Scripture readings such as psalms are in the voice of the people speaking to God) and other aspects, but the greater proportion of worship is of people speaking to God. Worship is a dialogue between God and his people, not a performance for his people. This simple notion that God is the royal audience in worship has numerous implications for our worship. For one, God's presence is the comprehensive reality of worship. Therefore, the invocation is the dramatic beginning of worship as it calls upon God to be present by "invoking" his name. We call upon him because he has promised to be our God and dwell in our midst (Lev. 26:12; Jer. 30:22).

I once had the opportunity to attend a luncheon where President Reagan spoke. It was in a large hotel ballroom with the familiar round tables and baked chicken meal. The sponsor was a business organization, so there was a lot of networking and work talk as we ate and awaited the President's arrival. At one point, almost imperceptibly, a hush began to pass across the ballroom before the exuberant announcement, "Ladies and gentlemen, the President of the United States!" at which point "Hail to the Chief" was struck by a small ensemble and the President strode onto the dais. Those gathered rose to their feet and erupted in applause, not just because the president was very popular, but because he was the guest of honor and, as we say, the leader of the free world. His arrival was dramatic.

God's presence among us in worship is the wonder of wonders. With Solomon we know that heaven and the highest heaven cannot contain God (1 Kings 8:27), but he regards the prayers of his servants. When Aaron raised his hands over Israel to pronounce the Aaronic blessing, he spoke for the God who was present among his people. Today, when we gather in Christ's name, we know that he has promised to be among us (Matt. 18:20). If we think of worship as a "concert of praise" with God as the royal audience, the invocation along with the call to worship is that moment when the conductor's baton is raised in the air while he gains the rapt attention of all the musicians and then provides the downbeat to begin. It should not be like the slow start of rousing a teenager from bed or the transformation from bleary-eyed to bushy-tailed that many adults experience with their first morning cup of coffee. The invocation is the entrance of the victorious King come to receive the praises of his subjects (Ps. 24:7–10).

If God is the royal audience present in our worship, then we are all the performers not just a select few musicians. Someone once described church as being like a major college football game—thousands of people desperately in need of exercise being entertained by twenty-two people desperately in need of rest. If there is one thing that could revolutionize worship more than anything else in our day, it would be reconceiving worship as participation rather than entertainment. Few people come to worship with the crass attitude that says "Entertain me!" yet there are ways that subtly indicate an entertainment dynamic has a strong influence in our congregations. The term "stage" is used to refer to the raised platform where worship leaders stand. Musicians refer to the morning's songs as "sets." Pastors sometimes refer to their listeners as an "audience." The simple use of these terms doesn't necessarily indicate the problem I am describing, but their usage potentially can. Most noticeable is when the choices of music and the way in which the music is performed inhibit singing by the congregation.

One of the ironies of the great proliferation of music in our day is that it has generally made us less musical. Worship music is increasingly conceded as the exclusive territory of the talented. Of course, the people aren't only to sing to God, but they are to come "addressing one another in psalms and hymns and spiritual songs, singing and making melody to the Lord with your heart" (Eph. 5:19; also Col. 3:16). While we sing to God, we are also to sing for the benefit and encouragement of one another. If we can't hear one another, then we can't provide this encouragement.

An entertainment attitude toward music can be just as true in a traditional-style service as in a contemporary one. This drift toward performance in music isn't new. By the time of Luther and the Reformation, not only had the church come to withhold the communion cup from the people, but the music of the church was largely the role of trained choirs. Just as Luther's reforms restored the cup to the people, he also resolved to return singing to them as well. Luther's success at promoting singing in the church and in the home led one Jesuit to say derisively, "Luther has murdered more souls with his songs than with his writings and sermons."[1] Music specialists who are not committed to participation as a fundamental principle will often remove singing from the lips of the people as music selection, complexity, and volume make it more difficult for the people to sing and to hear one another sing. This can happen with traditional as well as contemporary music genres and styles.

While contemporary worship is often blamed for the drift toward worship as entertainment, ironically, even some of those

---

1   Christopher Boyd Brown, *Singing the Gospel: Lutheran Hymns and the Success of the Reformation* (Cambridge, MA: Harvard University Press, 2005), 171.

who criticize contemporary worship undermine the participatory nature of worship by making worship sermon-centric. Churches that try to mitigate the outsized role of music by giving greater emphasis to the role of Scripture can also undermine the participatory nature of worship. For example, they can become clergy-centered in worship. In many churches in the Protestant "free worship" tradition the worshipers spend a disproportionate amount of time listening while only the pastor speaks, whether in prayer, Scripture reading, or preaching. The prayers become primarily prayers *for* the people rather than the prayers *of* the people. Free worship traditions also can become "sermon-centric" in their worship. The Scripture is "that word above all earthly power" through which the triune God makes known his will for us in and through Jesus Christ. We cannot overstate the precious privilege it is to hear God speak through his word. It is through his word that God continues to do his work in us and in the world. Yet disproportionate attention to the sermon devolves the throne room of worship into a classroom. Learning should and must take place in biblical worship, but learning alone does not constitute worship.

One prominent characteristic of nonparticipatory worship is the "exile of public prayer." Historically, Christian worship has consisted of a series of elements like the scenes in a play or the movements of a symphony. Taken together those elements comprised the drama of worship. Most of those movements consisted in prayer, whether sung or spoken. Prayer, along with God speaking to initiate prayer and responding to prayer, serves as the basic architecture of worship. In other words, the plot in the drama of participatory worship is prayer.

In many instances today, prayer serves only as a segue rather than the superstructure of worship and is often perfunctory or unplanned and led by persons with talents other than a knowledge of Scripture and prayer. This exile of prayer is largely attributable to the emergence of what James F. White has termed "frontier worship."[2] Also called "two-phase worship," it is the pattern that developed on the American frontier, where there were few established churches and Christian gatherings took on more of an evangelistic role. The pattern of frontier worship is usually a warm welcome followed by a series of songs that are to prepare the listeners for a message that has a strong evangelistic or renewal appeal calling for an emotional response. Sometimes a testimony came between the music and the message. Over the course of the twentieth century as parachurch ministries used this format, frontier worship worked its way into the worship patterns of many churches. However, just as pizza is often the standard menu of many youth gatherings, frontier worship doesn't provide a balanced diet. Like a proper meal, biblical worship serves all the food groups of worship and in an order that provides both a nutritious and delectable feast. Frontier worship, though not really worship, has its place in evangelistic meetings, but the church is impoverished when it displaces the dialogue between God and his people that a full menu of biblical prayer provides.

The displacement of the drama of redemption by this two-phase worship reflects a lack of confidence in what Edmund Clowney termed "doxological evangelism" of the kind reflected in 1 Corinthians 14.[3] There Paul describes the original "at-

2   James F. White, *Protestant Worship* (Atlanta: Westminster John Knox, 1989), 171–91.
3   Edmund P. Clowney, *The Church* (Downers Grove, IL: InterVarsity, 1995), 1.

tractional church" model. In commending an intelligibility that was not at the expense of doxology, he asserts that when "an unbeliever or outsider enters, he is convicted by all, he is called to account by all, the secrets of his heart are disclosed, and so, falling on his face, he will worship God and declare that God is really among you" (1 Cor. 14:24–25). This is the very kind of worship envisioned by the prophet Isaiah when the nations would be drawn to the mountain of the Lord (Isa. 2:2). The church of Jesus Christ is the city of God, the assembly of heaven, and the true Mount Zion to which the nations are being gathered (Heb. 12:22–23). The gospel is not to be heard only in the sermon, but the whole worship service should relate the drama of redemption. One vital way of telling the whole story is to include a full menu of prayer.

Restoring and maintaining a healthy worship diet involves learning and practicing all the prayer food groups. Two excellent resources on corporate prayer are Hughes Oliphant Old's *Leading in Prayer* and Matthew Henry's *A Way to Pray*.[4] Old's workbook is especially helpful for pastors and elders in defining, describing, and providing numerous examples of the different kinds of prayer that have historically comprised Christian worship. Henry's book is a compendium of Scripture verses formulated as prayers organized by a "method" that reflects the categories and order found in Old's book. Henry's book is a treasury of Scriptural prayers that will equip all Christians, especially heads of families and pastors, for conversation with God. First published in 1720, it appeared

---

4   Hughes Oliphant Old, *Leading in Prayer: A Workbook for Worship* (Grand Rapids, MI: Eerdmans, 1995), and Matthew Henry, *A Way to Pray: A Biblical Method for Enriching Your Prayer Life*, ed. O. Palmer Robertson (Carlisle, PA: Banner of Truth, 2020).

until recently under the title *A Method for Prayer with Scripture Expressions Proper to Be Used under Each Head*. An edition that includes the Scripture references and other resources on prayer is the most desirable to obtain. As Henry so well stated concerning prayer as the principal parts of worship,

> Besides your worshiping of God in secret, and in your families, which this must not supersede, or justle out, you here call upon God's name in a solemn assembly; and it is as much your business in all such exercises to pray a prayer together, as it is to hear a sermon . . .[5]

The Aaronic Blessing as Libretto

With this foundational understanding of prayer as the principal architecture of worship, we can now consider how our insight into the Aaronic blessing and its realization in the glory of God through the face of Christ can inform and enhance a typical worship service. God's gracious gaze can serve as a guide for reflecting upon and participating in the scenes of the drama. Perhaps you have been to a concert, where attendees are handed a libretto as they arrive. You pore over it before the concert to familiarize yourself with the musicians, the conductor, the composer, and the selections to be performed. Looking at worship through the lens of the Aaronic blessing is like a grand libretto for worship. The movements of this symphony, which we will consider, are the most common elements of the church's worship, similar to

5   Matthew Henry, "How to Begin Every Day with God," *A Method for Prayer with Scripture Expressions and Directions for Daily Communion with God*, ed. J. Ligon Duncan III (Greenville, SC: Reformed Academic Press, 1994), 256.

how certain musical forms such as requiems are comprised of certain standard movements.

Worship begins with a summons, a call to worship. Often a single verse of a psalm, the call to worship gathers the people of God not just physically, but for a common purpose. Like the steeple bell that my childhood church sexton, Mr. Sawyer, used to let me ring, the call peals the people. Envision Aaron with raised hands over the multitude of the *qāhāl*, the assembly, the Hebrew word that the New Testament renders as *ekklēsia*, "church." This blessing commissioned to Aaron wasn't administered from house to house, but over the gathered people of God. The Aaronic blessing reminds us that those who are blessed, from the smallest to the greatest (Ps. 115:13) are those who have responded to the call to "magnify the LORD with me" (Ps. 34:3). It is within the walls of Zion where God's mighty acts have saved his people that those acts are to be remembered and praised (Psalm 48).[6]

Though practices vary widely, a well-balanced liturgy should include the following elements:

Invocation—The invocation, as we have seen already, calls upon the triune God to be present and petitions him to receive our worship in and through Jesus Christ. The invocation names God as our God, which is the penultimate effect of the Aaronic blessing—"So shall they put my name upon the people of Israel, and I will bless them" (Num. 6:27). We gather in

---

6   For more on the connection between Zion and Jerusalem in the Old Testament and the church today, see Michael J. Glodo, "The Church in the Old Testament," *Westminster Society Journal 3: The Beauty of the Local Church*, Summer 2019: 63–80.

the presence of the triune God as those who have received his name in baptism.

Praise—God's presence is met with praise, principally for his attributes and his acts. In worship God blesses his people by conveying to them certain aspects of his nature, his "communicable attributes." These communicable attributes constitute the image into which we are being transformed (2 Cor. 3:18). The *shalom* we receive from God is derivative of God's nature. Praising God also includes celebrating his mighty acts of salvation. Israel's first act after crossing the Red Sea was to sing God's praise (Exodus 15) for God's mighty acts. Israel gathered under the outstretched arms of Aaron as those who had seen the mighty arm of God destroying the powers that bound them (Ex. 6:6; 15:16; Deut. 4:34; 5:15) and delivering them for the express purpose of worshiping him in freedom (Ex. 4:23; 7:16; 8:1, 20; 9:1). God's mighty acts have climaxed in the wonders he performed in and through Jesus Christ (Acts 2:22–24). Therefore, in and through Jesus Christ, we praise God for his inherent worthiness and his works that are reflected and anticipated in the Aaronic blessing.

Confession—Praise naturally leads to repentance. It is not possible to stand sensibly in the presence of God, giving him praise, without becoming aware of our own unworthy condition and actual transgressions. As the *Book of Common Prayer* familiarly reminds us, "we have sinned against [God] in thought, word, and deed, by what we have done, and by what we have left undone and have not loved God with our whole heart or our neighbors as ourselves."[7]

---

7 *The Book of Common Prayer* (New York: Church Hymnal Corporation), 331.

There are several ways in which the Aaronic blessing sheds light on confession of sin. First, when we recall the context of the blessing, we remember that the prerequisite to being in God's presence is being a saved and consecrated people. We only stand in the overwhelming presence of God's holiness because we have first been brought into his presence through his saving work in Christ. When we behold the glory of God in the face of Jesus Christ, we behold a glory perfected through Christ's suffering as he atoned for our sins. Second, the context of the blessing reminds us that those whom God has saved must consecrate themselves before him. Just as the assembly blessed by Aaron had consecrated itself through the gracious provisions of God's law, so we too must renew our devotion to the Lord every time we enter his presence.

The Son—Jesus Christ secures for us the promise of the Aaronic blessing. He rightly, then, has a central place in worship. He, along with the Father and the Spirit, is whom we worship. However, Christ, as the new *imago Dei*, is also our real worship leader. Hebrews 2:6–8 applies Psalm 8 to magnify the point that the Redeemer, to redeem those with a human nature, first took on a human nature. "For he who sanctifies and those who are sanctified all have one source" (Heb. 2:11). Jesus Christ is a sufficient Savior because he became a servant Savior in order to suffer, die, and rise on our behalf. He is also a "singing Savior," as indicated by the quote from Psalm 22:22, "I will tell of your name to my brothers; in the midst of the congregation I will sing your praise." As Edmund Clowney so memorably put it:

But now the risen Savior sings in glory. He is the sweet singer of Israel, the choirmaster of heaven. He is not ashamed to call us brethren, but sings in the midst of his assembled saints in the heavenly Zion and on earth where two or three are gathered in his name.[8]

Supplication—Confession is naturally made with or followed by supplication (prayers asking God for grace to change). In the Aaronic blessing, Aaron the high priest blessed the congregation. Aaron also faced toward God on behalf of the people. Even more so in Christ, the one who blesses us also intercedes for us (Heb. 7:25). In our prayers of supplication, we ask God by the Spirit to carry out the work of transforming us to be like Christ (2 Cor. 3:18) until we are fully like him (1 John 3:2).

Assurance—God's readiness to be gracious and shine his face upon his people is explicit in the Aaronic blessing. Therefore, the assurance of pardon pronounced by the minister or read from Scripture that follows the time of confession is a shining moment in worship. It's when God is gracious to his people. He is gracious because confession is done in the name of his righteous Son, in whose face the glory of God is reflected.

Thanksgiving—In response to the assurance of our pardon, we respond in gratitude with prayers of thanksgiving. In our thanksgiving, we can enumerate the blessings of the Aaronic blessing appropriate to their scope and depth as we learned in chapter 2.

---

8   Edmund P. Clowney, "The Singing Savior," *Moody Monthly*, July/August 1979: 41.

The Aaronic blessing can serve as an inventory of the richness of our inheritance in Christ so that we forget none of God's blessings (Ps. 103:2).

Intercession—Intercessory prayer, prayer for others, is an essential part of our calling as the people of God. As a royal priesthood and a holy nation (1 Pet. 2:9), God's people are to mediate the blessings of God to one another and to the nations by interceding. We only need to follow the arc from Aaron to Jesus Christ in order to see the perfection of that calling in Christ. Jesus is the reality, which Aaron symbolized in shadow, but Jesus is also of a greater priesthood than Aaron as part of the priestly order of Melchizedek (Hebrews 7) administering a new and better covenant than Aaron (Hebrews 8).

While there are prayers as part of the administration of the Lord's Supper, it's most immediately relevant to the Aaronic blessing and the beatific vision of Christ to point out that in the bread and the cup is where God makes himself visible to us. In the elements of communion, we are given sensible signs to look through and beyond with the eyes of faith. In the bread and the cup, by faith, we see the gracious gaze of God's face in Christ.

Benediction—The final act in the drama of Christian worship is the benediction. From elementary through high school I was in the school band. As a trombonist and bassist, I read and played my own parts as I heard the other parts playing around me. Every year the band director would choose seniors to assist in conducting, primarily for the pep band at basketball games but occasionally for a single piece during the spring concert. When I had the opportunity to conduct for the pep band, my director handed me the director's score to rehearse. The score had not only the part I had learned and played but all the parts for all the instruments. From that time on my own parts were more meaningful because I played them with greater awareness of the conductor's role. In that spirit, and for the benefit of ministers reading this book, we will consider the benediction in worship through the eyes of the minister. If you are a layperson, this overview can be a rare opportunity for you to "look at the conductor's score" so that the insights can enrich your own participation in worship.

The Ministry of Benediction

Whenever I have returned to my hometown for my high school class reunion, it seems I have always been asked to perform the clerical function of getting everyone quiet before the meal and saying the obligatory before-meal prayer. Mindful that some of my classmates may not have thought of me as clergy material during my high school days, I try hard not to come off as pretentious. One year, after I performed the clerical function of getting everyone to stop talking, I prefaced my prayer by saying, "I'm a professional. Don't try this at home." My attempted humor earned me a groan or two but mostly confused looks. Obviously, the fact that pastors often pray in their professional roles shouldn't dissuade all Christians from praying. So why is it customary in most churches for the minister to pronounce the benediction?

There is a broad range of beliefs and a lot of confusion today about what is and isn't the minister's job. In some traditions ministers or priests are perceived as a separate class of Christians whose roles are indispensable to the Christian life. In other traditions, the minister is just one among equals, distinguished only by getting a paycheck from the church. In some traditions, there is a complete disavowal of there being anything like ordained clergy. To comprehend and appropriate the benediction, we must be clear on just who is pronouncing it.

Among Protestants, a common source of confusion or even tension about the role of the minister arises from a basic misunderstanding of the Reformation. The Reformation was notable, among many things, for recovering the belief in the priesthood of all believers. As we can see from comparing Exodus 19:6 and 1 Peter 2:9, all God's people are priests, not just a select group. Yet those sixteenth- and seventeenth-century Reformers who did so much to revive the gospel of justification by grace alone through faith alone and who spoke so fiercely against the errors and abuses in medieval Roman Catholicism did not dispense with a high view of the office of minister while they worked to recover the doctrine of the priesthood of all believers. Except for the Anabaptists (not the same as Baptists), the Reformers agreed with how the Second Helvetic Confession expressed this. After acknowledging that "the first beginning, institution, and office of ministers is a most ancient arrangement of God himself, and not a new one of men,"[9] this confession goes on to explain the relationship of the ministry to the priesthood of all believers.

PRIESTHOOD OF ALL BELIEVERS. To be sure, Christ's apostles call all who believe in Christ "priests," but not on account of an office, but because, all the faithful having been made

9 Second Helvetic Confession, Chapter XVIII, "Of the Ministers of the Church and Their Duties."

kings and priests, we are able to offer up a spiritual sacrifices to God through Christ (Ex. 19:6; 1 Peter 2:9; Rev. 1:6). Therefore, the priesthood and the ministry are very different from one another. For the priesthood, as we have just said, is common to all Christians; not so is the ministry. Nor have we abolished the ministry of the Church because we have repudiated the papal priesthood from the Church of Christ.[10]

In our populist contemporary culture with its emphasis on individualism, this might sound like a novel idea to many evangelical Christians. Even in traditions whose official doctrine upholds this understanding of the minister's office, there is often great effort on the part of pastors to communicate that they are just regular people like everyone else. In many ways they are the same as everyone else, but in their office they do have a unique role in their churches. From the days of Moses up through the New Testament, we can observe the practice of God's people setting apart certain persons for distinct roles and authority (Ex. 18:19–27; Num. 11:16–30; 27:22–23; Acts 13:2; 1 Tim. 5:22; 2 Tim. 1:6). Besides the long-established practice, pastors are specifically mentioned as among the offices given to the church by the ascended Christ (Eph. 4:8–13). Chief among the special tasks given to ministers is to speak for God.

As each has received a gift, use it to serve one another, as good stewards of God's varied grace: whoever speaks, as one who speaks oracles of God; . . . (1 Pet. 4:10–11)

---

10 Second Helvetic Confession, Chapter XVIII, "Of the Ministers of the Church and Their Duties."

In speaking for God, ministers don't just speak about God. They are actually God's means of speaking to his church (Rom. 10:14–17). When God's word is preached, it is Christ himself who is heard and believed.[11]

From the beginning God did things by his word. In creation, he spoke and "it was" (Genesis 1; Heb. 1:3). Jesus raised Lazarus from the dead by his word (John 11:43). The apostolic preaching of the gospel was received as the very word of God (1 Thess. 2:13) and was how believers were born again (1 Pet. 1:23). While there are certain qualifiers and cautions that must accompany this doctrine, such as the need for preachers to be biblical and to be authorized by the church, Reformation believers universally believed that

THE PREACHING OF THE WORD OF GOD IS THE WORD OF GOD. Wherefore when this Word of God is now preached in the church by preachers lawfully called, we believe that the very Word of God is proclaimed, and received by the faithful; and that neither any other Word of God is to be invented nor is to be expected from heaven: and that now the Word itself which is preached is to be regarded, not the minister that preaches; for even if he be evil and a sinner, nevertheless the Word of God remains still true and good.[12]

---

11 For full expositions of this passage see John Calvin, *Commentaries on the Epistle of Paul the Apostle to the Romans*, trans. John Owen (Grand Rapids, MI: Baker, 1984), 399; Leon Morris, *The Epistle to the Romans* (Downers Grove, IL: InterVarsity Press, 1988), 390; and John Murray, *The Epistle to the Romans*, New International Commentary on the New Testament (Grand Rapids, MI: Eerdmans, 1968), 2:58.

12 Second Helvetic Confession, Chapter I, "Of the Holy Scriptures Being the True Word of God."

The biblical understanding of the minister's role and preaching helps us to understand that in certain actions, the minister is not simply speaking about God or praying to God but speaking God's words on God's behalf as God's servant. The benediction is just such a word because the minister is speaking a word from God. Just as Aaron was charged to speak the Aaronic blessing over the assembly on God's behalf, Christ's ministers speak a word from God when pronouncing the benediction. Since God's word is God's deed, this means the benediction is more than a prayer. It's what speech theorists term a "performative word," a word that by nature is an action. For example, the very statement that God's face shines upon us, spoken by the command of God, is the way that God's face shines on us. Or similar to how Jesus's rebuke of the wind and the waves calmed the sea (Mark 4:39), when the benediction pronounces "peace" (2 Thess. 3:16), the very word "peace" can powerfully calm our hearts. As with every word from God, a benediction will not return to God void but accomplish God's purpose (Isa. 55:11).

So holding both the truth that all God's people are priests and the truth that Christ's ministers are speaking on behalf of God, who should pronounce the benediction over a congregation? I'd answer that just as with the preaching of the word, the benediction should only be pronounced by those who have been authorized through proper qualifications to speak God's word. It is true that in many churches preaching is not limited to ordained ministers. Not all churches practice this, just as not all churches limit the preaching of the word to those who have been called, trained, and set apart for the work. A minister's and a church's view on who should pronounce the benediction will parallel their view of who should preach God's word.

The Minister's Manner

What one believes about the nature of the benediction should then determine the manner in which the minister pronounces the benediction. I believe he should not be a trumpet with an "uncertain sound," to borrow a phrase from the King James Version of 1 Corinthians 14:8. While our sermons may be more or less clear, there is no excuse for a benediction not to ring out. Clarity is the consequence of confidence, competence, and preparation. A minister should not only have the confidence that he speaks a word of blessing on behalf of God, but he should be practiced enough to be competent. Following the model of my late professor Robert S. Rayburn, I require my preaching students to memorize five different benedictions so they don't have to stare down at their Bible, or worse, a smart phone while pronouncing the blessing over the congregation. The all-too-common image of a pastor pronouncing a benediction with one hand raised, one hand holding a text, with his eyes down is something I've come to call a "subway rider benediction" for it resembles a busy commuter holding a ceiling strap while reading the newspaper. The minister, in the tradition of Aaron, the synagogue, and the ancient church, should raise both hands over his head and look the people in the eye. Memorizing several classic benedictions provides competence, and intentionally planning ahead provides preparation. One particular benediction or another might be appropriate to specific occasions. Otherwise, I'd advise a regular rotation.

Since the benediction is a word spoken by God through his minister, it is not a prayer. Therefore, I believe the minister should say before declaring the blessing, "Lift your eyes to receive the blessing of God!" After all, God's blessing is the promise of his face shining upon us and his countenance lifted upon us. If the God of Isaiah's vision looks upon us in blessing, by what logic should the people close their eyes or stare at the floor? Many congregations have begun the practice of holding open hands with palms up during the benediction. While this might be conducive to a receptive attitude, the open eyes are more explicitly in keeping with the image of the Aaronic blessing. Granted, there are those who have been taught that ministers don't have any special role, or who through habit may continue to turn their faces to the floor when God's face is shining on them. All a pastor can do is gently and clearly continue to invite these worshipers to meet God's gaze. The minister likewise should look his people in the eye, scanning the congregation to make as much eye contact as possible while heralding God's blessing.

William Willimon, former dean of the chapel at Duke Divinity School and now professor of the practice of Christian ministry, shares a conversation he had that should encourage pastors in this ministry. A woman was expressing to him her delight with her new pastor. When asked why she liked him so, she replied, "He gives the best benedictions." When asked to elaborate, she went on,

> Well, we had never thought much about benedictions. Perhaps we had never really done one. But the first Sunday he was with us, at the conclusion of the worship service, rather than rush back to the door to greet everyone, he stayed at the front and said something like: "Now I am going to bless you. I want you all to look at me and receive my blessing because you may really need it next week." We all watched and as he raised both hands

high above his head, stretching out as if to embrace us, looking at each one of us, and almost like a father, blessing us in the name of the Father, and of the Son, and of the Holy Spirit. His benedictions have become the highlight of each Sunday as far as I am concerned.[13]

Willimon goes on to express his frustration with pastors who are less zealous about benedictions and refers to an article by clinical psychologist Paul Pruyser who "was disturbed at the half-hearted way in which many pastors pronounce benedictions."[14] Willimon, summarizing Pruyser, posits two sources for the decline from within their mainline denomination context. The first posited cause is "an erosion of the classical theological doctrine of providence." As a "symbol of providence," the benediction rests upon the belief that God is guiding and directing the affairs of the world, not a fashionable belief in an age that precludes the supernatural and tries to explain everything via science. The second reason for decline is pastors' loss of confidence in their calling. That is, pastors have lost confidence in the belief that the office of minister is an instrumental means by which God materially acts in the world.

These two observations are just as applicable to a conservative Protestant context as they are to a mainline context, particularly the latter reason. The populism inherent in evangelical belief

13 William H. Willimon, *Worship as Pastoral Care* (Nashville, TN: Abingdon, 1979), 210.
14 Paul W. Pruyser, "The Master Hand: Psychological Notes on Pastoral Blessing," in *The New Shape of Pastoral Theology: Essays in Honor of Seward Hiltner*, ed. William B. Oglesby, Jr. (Nashville, TN: Abingdon, 1969), 352–65, cited in Willimon, *Worship as Pastoral Care*, 211.

inherently carries with it a desire for the pastor to convince his congregation that he is no different than they, or as Willimon puts it, "one of the boys." The laying aside of clerical gowns in exchange for the business suit, and now the business suit in exchange for untucked shirts and torn jeans, reflects a decline in belief in the office of minister. Authenticity, the contemporary currency for authority, requires expressing self-doubt and self-abasement. Ironically, Willimon notes, "There is a kind of incipient clericalism behind our efforts to appear to be non-leaders of the community's worship."[15] Willimon is right to argue that we as ministers have no right to make little of that which the church historically has made much.

To put things more colloquially, it takes ministerial guts to look people in the eye, pronounce the benediction, and believe that God is using us in that moment to effect a real change in the hearts of our people and in the world outside the church door. Our confidence is not in the flesh, but in the foolish medium of the ministry through which God has decided to shame the wisdom of the world. As the Second Helvetic Confession states, "It is true that God can, by his power, without any means join to himself a Church from among men; but he preferred to deal with men by the ministry of men."[16] Unfortunately, "in common practice, a Benediction may simply be the perfunctory close to a worship service, but with skilled attention a Benediction can be a powerful instrument of pastoral care."[17] And so,

---

15 Willimon, *Worship as Pastoral Care*, 213.
16 Second Helvetic Confession, Chapter XVIII, "Of the Ministers of the Church and Their Duties."
17 Bryan Chapell, *Christ-Centered Worship: Letting the Gospel Shape Our Worship* (Grand Rapids, MI: BakerAcademic, 2009), 254.

In this final act of worship, the pastor blesses the people before they scatter. The blessing is not a prayer; it is a farewell word from the pastor to the congregation in God's name. Therefore, it should be done audibly in front of the congregation with arms outstretched as if to embrace the congregation, or with hands raised over the people.[18]

Choosing Benedictions

There is a range of beliefs and practices when it comes to choosing the words of the benediction. I believe it is wise to limit oneself to the handful of Scripture passages that are explicit blessings rather than trying to make passages of Scripture that were not originally benedictions into benedictions. Whenever I encounter suitable texts as I read Scripture, I jot the reference in the back pages of my Bible. With the ones I use most frequently in bold, here is my list:

Numbers 6:24–26
Psalm 121:7–8
Romans 15:5–6
Romans 15:13
Romans 15:33
Romans 16:20
1 Corinthians 16:23
2 Corinthians 13:14
Galatians 6:18
Ephesians 6:23–24
Philippians 4:19–20

18 William H. Willimon, *A Guide to Preaching and Leading Worship* (Louisville, KY: Westminster John Knox Press, 2008), 23.

Philippians 4:23
Colossians 4:18
Philemon 25
1 Thessalonians 3:12–13
1 Thessalonians 5:23–24
2 Thessalonians 2:16–17
2 Thessalonians 3:5
2 Thessalonians 3:16
1 Timothy 6:21
2 Timothy 4:22
Hebrews 13:20–21
1 Peter 5:14b
2 Peter 1:2
2 John 3
Revelation 22:21

The difference between benedictions and salutations is not always definitive. Many lists will include salutations which are not, strictly speaking, benedictions. There are a variety of published works that provide similar catalogs of benedictions.[19] As indicated by Bryan Chapell, in addition to these common benedictions, many pastors will combine scriptural texts, adapt scriptural texts, and even use non-scriptural texts such as hymn portions, sacred poetry, or other suitable phrases for the benediction.[20]

---

19 Robert I. Vasholz, *Benedictions: A Pocket Resource*, rev. ed. (Fearn, Ross-shire, UK: Christian Focus, 2015); and Ryan Kelly, *Calls to Worship, Invocations, and Benedictions* (Phillipsburg, NJ: P&R, 2022).
20 Bryan Chapell, *Christ-Centered Worship: Letting the Gospel Shape Our Practice* (Grand Rapids, MI: Baker Academic, 2017), 252. For examples of composed benedictions,

I believe a regular rotation of the most well-known scriptural benedictions is the best policy for three reasons. First, as explicit blessings, their language clearly conveys their function to the congregation. They don't get muddled into a stew of blessings, charges, salutations, and doxologies. Their function is clear, and they are not Scripture twisted in order to give the pastor a final chance to clarify his sermon. Second, the regular repetition of a small number reinforces the habituation of a liturgy. Constant innovation and variation, while possibly (though not assuredly) keeping worshipers attentive, does not catechize believers into well-formed habits of life. This benefit is one of the helpful points of James K. A. Smith's work on cultural liturgies, which argues we are much more creatures of habit than "brains on a stick."[21] Third, biblical benedictions school God's people in the language of Zion. When the prayers of worship, benedictions, and other elements are rehearsed over time, God's people are sealed more and more into their citizenship in the city of God by linguistic competency in their mother tongue of Scripture.

And One More Thing . . .

In many congregations the benediction is not the final word of worship. In fact, there are two additional words that are appropriate, both of which are God's desired responses to his blessing.

---

see Dale Ralph Davis, *Grace Be with You: Benedictions from Dale Ralph Davis* (Fearn, Ross-shire, Scotland: Christian Focus, 2019).

21 Such as James K. A. Smith, *You Are What You Love: The Spiritual Power of Habit* (Grand Rapids, MI: Brazos Press, 2016).

Doxology—A doxology is a word of praise spoken or, more commonly, sung by the congregation in response to God's blessing. God is the "blessed" God (1 Tim. 1:11; 6:15), "blessed" being the Greek *makarios*, such as in the Beatitudes. He is the one who is blessed, or "happy" within himself. Yet he shares that blessedness, he imparts his blessed life, to his people. "Blessed is the man" whose delight is in God's law (Psalm 1). "Blessed is the one whose transgression is forgiven" (Ps. 32:1). In worship we are called to "forget not all his benefits" (Ps. 103:2). God blesses us with his blessedness so that we might bless (Greek, *eulogeō*) his name in response. Therefore, a divinely intended purpose of God's blessing is for us to speak a blessing to him in return.

Charge—Our blessing by God is also to bring blessing upon the nations. Therefore, another final element of worship might be a charge to the people to go on mission. God blesses us with his blessedness so that we might bless him in return, but the blessed state of God's people is not theirs to keep to themselves. We are to share his blessedness. God promised to bless Abram when he called him out of Ur and to bless the nations through Abram (Gen. 12:1–3). The God of Abram showed himself from the beginning as a God who blesses in Melchizedek's benediction, "Blessed be Abram by God Most High" (Gen. 14:19). As a royal priesthood, God's people are to mediate his blessings to the world so that all for whom Christ died will share in the blessing promised to Abraham. Therefore, a proper conclusion to worship would be a charge on God's behalf such as, "Go in peace to love and serve the risen Lord Jesus Christ." The benediction can serve as the basis for our commission to be Christ's witnesses in the world. In Jesus's final moments with his disciples on earth, he commissioned them, but he also blessed them. Many scholars believe that Jesus's last words to his disciples were those of the Aaronic blessing. If so, it is fitting that our response to God's benediction should be going forth in Jesus's name on Jesus's mission.

> And he led them out as far as Bethany, and lifting up his hands he blessed them. While he blessed them, he parted from them and was carried up into heaven. And they worshiped him and returned to Jerusalem with great joy, and were continually in the temple blessing God. (Luke 24:50–53)

Conclusion

Having taught Old Testament for twenty years, I used to get asked from time to time if I had ever been to the Holy Land. Given how many lay Christians have visited Israel and its surroundings, I usually felt a little sheepish saying that I had not but that I had seen a lot of pictures. Sometimes the person asking would then begin telling me all about his trip. During that time there actually existed a tourist site in my city called "The Holy Land Experience," though I hadn't visited it either. I have friends who were personally acquainted with Jesus—that is, the theme park cast member who played him. Eventually, as a (stereo)typical professor who attempts to make a lesson out of everything, I came up with what I thought was a more clever response. I eventually began to answer by saying "Yes! I was there last Sunday!"

What made the land of Old Testament Israel holy was the special presence of her holy God. While we look forward to the day when the "the earth will be filled with the knowledge of the glory of the LORD as the waters cover the sea" (Hab. 2:14), God doesn't dwell in that theophanic presence with a particular nation today. Nevertheless, where two or three gather in the name of Jesus, he has promised to be among them (Matt. 18:20) because "the Lord is the Spirit, and where the Spirit of the Lord is, there is freedom" (2 Cor. 3:17). When I answer the question as I now do, I'm not being cheeky (well, maybe a little . . .), I'm being biblical. The risen Christ by the Spirit is present when Christ's assembly, the church, gathers in his name. By our union with Christ, we are both in heaven gathered around the throne of God (Eph. 2:6; Col. 3:1) and gathered bodily, in our bodies with faces, here on earth. The author of Hebrews says nothing less. Although all the Old Testament people who lived by faith "did not receive what was promised" (Heb. 11:39), we

> have come to Mount Zion and to the city of the living God, the heavenly Jerusalem, and to innumerable angels in festal gathering, and to the assembly of the firstborn who are enrolled in heaven, and to God, the judge of all, and to the spirits of the righteous made perfect, and to Jesus, the mediator of a new covenant, and to the sprinkled blood that speaks a better word than the blood of Abel. (Heb. 12:22–24)

We have come to the place that those Old Testament saints only welcomed from afar because Christ himself has entered that place as our great high priest (Heb. 9:11; 10:12, 25; 12:2).

The beatific vision of seeing God face-to-face at death and the eternal beatitude of the new heavens and earth are visions of faith that sustain believers in this earthly life. Yet as blissful as those future visions are, in the public worship of God through his regular means of grace we have access to God's presence along with the fullness of his promises in Jesus Christ. Even though we don't see all things subjected to Christ the way we will one day see them (Heb. 2:8), through the word and Spirit we see him with the eyes of faith (2:9). Even though we are still on our journey from this world to the world to come (Heb. 4:8–13), "pilgrims through this barren land," by faith we can enter God's sabbath rest if we don't neglect to meet together to encourage one another. The Aaronic blessing, now ours in the fullness of the glory of God in the face of Jesus Christ, can serve as the overture of the church's worship as we hear its refrains in all that we do in worship.

For Further Reflection

1. How do (or can) the prayers of worship tell the story of the gospel?

2. Consider the various steps of worship in your church and how they reflect different aspects of the Aaronic blessing as fulfilled in the glory of God in the face of Christ.

3. The next time you are in public worship, self-consciously think about responding in faith by believing the words of the benediction.

Conclusion

THE COVID-19 PANDEMIC WROUGHT a lot of confusion as well as suffering. It also has taught and will continue to teach us many things about human nature, including our own. Among its many lessons the pandemic has taught us that faces are important. The wearing or non-wearing of masks produced visceral responses of all kinds, ranging from those who refused to wear masks at all to those who regarded masks as moral imperatives. For some people, the presence or absence of masks became indicators of religious, social, intellectual, and moral virtue. One intriguing but unsettling reaction was from people who planned on continuing to wear their masks even if the risk of infection went away. These people were retail workers who prefer to not smile at customers, a retiree who was weary of the pressure to appear happy all the time, and a woman who felt both emotional freedom and freedom from the male gaze.[1]

Like real-life Queen Oruals in *Till We Have Faces*, people have become more attuned, even if subconsciously, to how faces reveal

---

1   Jeffrey H. Anderson, "The Masking of America: Faceless People Make Compliant Subjects, Not Good Citizens," *Claremont Review of Books* (Summer 2021), accessed July 8, 2022, https://claremontreviewofbooks.com.

and conceal and how masks and veils affect those around us. The importance of faces supports the idea that God made us with faces so that his could shine on ours. Seeing and being seen by God is the acme of human existence.

> One thing have I asked of the LORD,
>   that will I seek after:
> that I may dwell in the house of the LORD
>   all the days of my life,
> to gaze upon the beauty of the LORD
>   and to inquire in his temple. (Ps. 27:4)

This is why God graciously shines his face upon ours as promised in the Aaronic blessing and fulfilled in the glory of God reflected in the face of Jesus Christ.

C. S. Lewis's Queen Orual finally came to the answer that she had demanded from the gods. Her old teacher the Fox had long taught her that until we truly know what our questions are, what is truly in us, the gods will never answer us. As Orual realized, "How can they meet us face to face till we have faces?"[2] In other words, the gods will never answer until we come out from behind our masks and veils. When Orual's demand for answers finally brought "the god" near, her answer came. "I know now, Lord, why you utter no answer. You are yourself the answer. Before your face questions die away."[3] The good news of the gospel is not "till we have faces," but that we still have faces upon which God's face shines on ours in Christ.

2   C. S. Lewis, *Till We Have Faces: A Myth Retold* (New York: HarperOne, 2017), 335.
3   Lewis, *Till We Have Faces*, 351.

We all, like Orual, make masks and veils—veils to cover what is there, masks to project what is not. Veils hide us from others. Masks create the fictional characters we or others wish us to be. Both draw a curtain between us and the other image bearers of God, whether strangers, acquaintances, friends, or lovers. The good news is that the God of Aaron makes his face shine on us in Jesus Christ and fulfills the psalmist's longing for the beatific vision, rending the veil from top to bottom that separated us from God. It also has drawn back the curtain that otherwise hangs between us and our neighbors, from the most intimate neighbor to the stranger at our gates.

In wearing masks and veils, like Orual, we become like the gods of human making, and consequently lose our humanity.[4] The result, as Psalm 115 so strikingly warns us, is that we become lifeless and impotent like our idols (115:8). Alternatively, in the acme of human blessedness held forth in the Aaronic benediction, God unmasks his face to shine on ours. He shows his face in favor and invites us to uncover ours. The covering and masking of our faces makes us less human, but the revelation of God's face can make us fully human. Through Jesus Christ, we may now say with Isaiah, "My eyes have seen the King, the LORD of hosts!" (Isa. 6:5).

The heart of the gospel is not simply that we take off our masks and veils, but that God has shown his face in the face of Christ

---

4 This conclusion is adapted from a chapel sermon at Reformed Theological Seminary Orlando in December 2020, which developed into an article-length treatment 'We Still Have Faces' in *Reformed Faith and Practice* that same month, excerpts of which are included here by permission. Glodo, "We Still Have Faces," *Reformed Faith & Practice* 5, no. 3 (December 2020), 10–19.

and looked upon us to bless us and give us peace. Therefore, we must long for God's look as our greatest desire. We must look at ourselves as God has looked upon us and look at others in the same way. God made us with faces so his could shine on ours. God looks on us so that we must look differently at ourselves and at others. Let us long for the face of God in Christ so that we may look differently at ourselves and at others.

In my first ordained call as an assistant pastor over thirty-five years ago, on my first day, my pastor gave me a list of church members I needed to visit in their homes. My main responsibilities were outreach, evangelism, and assimilation, so I didn't quite see how visiting shut-ins would contribute to my effectiveness. Nevertheless, after a bit of procrastination I made my first appointment to visit Francis Finley. I was cautioned that she was battling a cancer that had required the removal of sinus and facial tissue and bone, but that with advance notice she would be prepared by putting on her prosthesis to hide the open cavity in her face. She had prepared tea and cookies before my arrival, and we had a visit that left me greatly impressed with her faith, humility, and kindness. I knew then why my pastor had sent me. The conversation was not easy because her surgeries had left her sinuses open, making it difficult for her to speak clearly, such as in the case of someone with an extreme cleft palate. But her kindness and incipient trust in God's care made me the more blessed from that conversation.

On my second visit a few months later, Mrs. Finley came to the door as before, but as I entered her home I was momentarily unnerved by the absence of her prosthesis. During the initial part of our conversation, I averted my gaze from her face, partly because of her appearance and partly because I wanted to dignify her by not staring at the gaping hole. After a few moments I had the same epiphany as I did some three decades later at the bedside of my father-in-law, that she deserved to be looked in the eyes the way she had been all the years before her cancer. Those bright, Irish eyes that had been looking in my eyes the whole time were still lively, reflecting an unshakable faith. Soon her whole face was within the frame of my gaze because her whole face, not just her eyes, were her. For me it became something of a beatific vision, not of the unseen God, but of an image of God himself upon whom he had lifted his countenance and given peace. Mrs. Finley epitomized someone who lived and died before the face of God.

> Hear, O LORD, when I cry aloud;
>> be gracious to me and answer me!
> You have said, "Seek my face."
> My heart says to you,
>> "Your face, LORD, do I seek." (Ps. 27:7–8)

Anne Cousin's nineteenth-century hymn "The Sands of Time Are Sinking" envisions the day when we shall see him face-to-face (1 Cor. 13:12). As the second verse says, "The king there in his beauty, without a veil is seen" and "glory, glory dwelleth in Emmanuel's land." Not only then, but even now, the fourth verse should guide us:

> The bride eyes not her garment,
> But her dear Bridegroom's face;
> I will not gaze at glory
> But on my King of grace.

Not at the crown He giveth
But on His pierced hand;
The Lamb is all the glory
Of Emmanuel's land.[5]

May we long for the look of God's countenance lifted on us. May we, since God has so graciously invited us to seek his face and has answered our cry in the face of Jesus Christ, may we say yes from the heart, "Your face, Lord, do I seek." And may we not only then look at ourselves differently, but look at others in Jesus's name.

5   Anne R. Cousin, "The Sands of Time Are Sinking," *Trinity Hymnal*, rev. ed. (Atlanta: Great Commission Publications, 1997), no. 546.

Appendix

A Liturgy of God's Gracious Gaze

IN CHAPTER 6 WE LEARNED how the Aaronic blessing can function as an overture to the symphony of worship. The following material is a suggested order of worship that draws explicitly upon the Aaronic blessing and its related themes. While all these elements may not necessarily be included in a single worship service, they are provided for possible inclusion. Several elements are accompanied by "prefaces" in *italics* which are explanations and introductions the leader might speak to the congregation to guide their participation. The prayers could be unison, leader-led, or responsive.

Call to Worship

Hear the psalmist's resolute commitment to praise with his invitation to those who will humble themselves before the Lord.

> I will bless the LORD at all times;
>> his praise shall continually be in my mouth.

My soul makes its boast in the LORD;
　　let the humble hear and be glad.
Oh, magnify the LORD with me,
　　and let us exalt his name together!

I sought the LORD, and he answered me
　　and delivered me from all my fears.
Those who look to him are radiant,
　　and their faces shall never be ashamed. (Ps. 34:1–5)

Invocation

Having gathered together for the purpose of praise, let us call upon God to be in our midst. As the psalmist has said:

One thing have I asked of the LORD,
　　that will I seek after:
that I may dwell in the house of the LORD
　　all the days of my life,
to gaze upon the beauty of the LORD
　　and to inquire in his temple (Ps. 27:4)

Lord, it is our heart's desire to behold your beauty within your sanctuary as you have made us a temple of the Holy Spirit. Heaven is your throne and the earth your footstool; you dwell in a high and holy place, yet as a kingdom of priests and a holy nation, we ask you to dwell on earth with us by your Spirit that you would draw near to us in the beauty of your holiness as we give you the glory due your name. In the name of your Son and our Savior, Jesus Christ, we pray. Amen.

Hymn

Children of God, let us "stand in awe before his face" to unite our hearts and voices in praise for our triune God as we sing together.

"All You That Fear Jehovah's Name"

Reading of the Law

[**Note:** The reading of the law preceding confession of sin, while often from the Ten Commandments or the Sermon on the Mount, is not limited to specific commands in Scripture. Reading the law can be based upon any passage through which the norm of God's law convicts us of sin and drives us to God's mercy in Christ (Gal. 3:24).]

Hear the law of God as it is found for us in the prophet Isaiah 6:1–5:

In the year that King Uzziah died I saw the Lord sitting upon a throne, high and lifted up; and the train of his robe filled the temple. Above him stood the seraphim. Each had six wings: with two he covered his face, and with two he covered his feet, and with two he flew. And one called to another and said:

"Holy, holy, holy is the LORD of hosts;
the whole earth is full of his glory!"

And the foundations of the thresholds shook at the voice of him who called, and the house was filled with smoke. And I said:

"Woe is me! For I am lost; for I am a man of unclean lips, and I dwell in the midst of a people of unclean lips; for my eyes have seen the King, the Lord of hosts!"

Confession

Even as we have bid God to come in the beauty of holiness, as we behold him face-to-face we are undone; for the glory of God's presence causes us, like the prophet, to cry out, "Woe is me!" Let us unite our hearts and voices together as we confess our uncleanness. Let us confess our sin.

There is no one who calls upon your name,
    who rouses himself to take hold of you;
for you have hidden your face from us,
    and have made us melt in the hand of our iniquities.
      (Isa. 64:7)

Hear, O Lord, when we cry aloud;
    be gracious to me and answer me!
You have said, "Seek my face."
My heart says to you,
"Your face, Lord, do I seek."
    Hide not your face from me.
Turn not your servants away in anger,
    O you who have been my help.
Cast me not off; forsake me not,
    O God of my salvation! (Ps. 27:7–9)

If you, O Lord, should mark iniquities,
 O Lord, who could stand?
But with you there is forgiveness,
 that you may be feared. (Ps. 130:3–4)

We pray to you in the name of the one who has clean hands and a
pure heart, who when tempted as we are, did not lift up his soul to
what is false or swear deceitfully, the righteous one Jesus Christ. And
as we pray, we do so in faith that

[God] has not despised or abhorred
 the affliction of the afflicted,
and he has not hidden his face from him,
 but has heard, when he cried to him. (Ps. 22:24)

Assurance/Declaration of Pardon (Sung or Read)

Hear, people, this word of assurance to all who have truly repented
of their sins and looked in faith to the saving work of Jesus Christ:

I sought the Lord, and he answered me
 and delivered me from all my fears.
Those who look to him are radiant,
and their faces shall never be ashamed. (Ps. 34:4–5)

[**Note:** In some traditions the minister declares the pardon using
scriptural language, while in others the pardon may be pronounced
or assured with the reading of an appropriate Scripture text such

as Psalm 17:15; 2 Corinthians 3:17 paired with Romans 8:1–2; or Jude 24–25.]

Supplication

[**Note:** Supplication, prayer for God's sanctifying grace, can be enfolded into confession or prayed separately before or after the assurance. For the justified person, dwelling in the presence of God is transformative and can be expressed by quoting or formulating prayer around such passages as Psalm 4:6.]

As we appeal to you on the merits of your Son, Jesus Christ, and his atoning death for our sins,

> There are many who say, "Who will show us some good?
> Lift up the light of your face upon us, O LORD!"
> You have put more joy in my heart
> than they have when their grain and wine abound.
> (Ps. 4:6–7)

Therefore we ask that as we look upon the glory of God in the face of Jesus Christ by your Spirit, that you would transform us from one degree of glory into another so that when we see him, we shall be like him. In Christ's name we pray. Amen.

Hymn/Song of Contrition or Assurance

In the assurance of God's pardon for those who truly repent of their sins and put their faith in Christ's atoning work, let us appeal in song to God for his transforming mercies in order to make us more and more into the image of his Son and our Savior.

"Jesus, Cast a Look on Me"

or

"Here, O My Lord, I See You Face to Face"

[**Note:** This category of hymn/song is also suitable for communion preparation.]

Thanksgiving

[**Note:** While the Old Testament sacrifices gave a prominent role to atonement, there were also numerous non-atonement offerings used to express gratitude and dedication to the Lord. Because Christian worship places great emphasis on the atoning work of Christ, we sometimes risk neglecting the proportion that gratitude is to have. Thanksgiving should have a prominent place in worship, thanks not just for God's pardon but for his provision, protection, and other blessings such that our gratitude extends beyond public worship into our everyday lives.]

With gratitude for God's gracious power and provisions for us, let us bring our offerings of thanks before him as he dwells in our midst.

Open to me the gates of righteousness,
    that I may enter through them
    and give thanks to the LORD.
This is the gate of the LORD;

the righteous shall enter through it.
I thank you that you have answered me
    and have become my salvation.
The stone that the builders rejected
    has become the cornerstone.
This is the Lord's doing;
    it is marvelous in our eyes.
This is the day that the Lord has made;
    let us rejoice and be glad in it. (Ps. 118:19–24)

Intercession

God himself has invited us to seek his face. Let us respond to his gracious invitation by seeking his grace for our needs and the needs of others.

[**Note:** Intercessory prayer for the needs of others is the ministry of the priesthood of all believers who stand before his gracious gaze, whether guided by a leader or by allowing members of the congregation to pray aloud.]

We believe with the psalmist that we shall look upon the goodness of the Lord in the land of the living, for you, O Lord, are good and do good.

The Reading of God's Word

[**Note:** Appropriate preaching texts could include all or portions of 2 Corinthians 3:1–4:6, any of the passages discussed in John 3, the transfiguration narratives (Matt. 17:1–8; Mark 9:2–8;

Luke 9:28–36), or a Gospel narrative in which Christ "saw" or otherwise engaged in a deeply personal encounter with someone who became an object of his mercy (e.g., Mark 5:21–43).]

Prayer for Illumination

[**Note:** In our natural state we do not have eyes to see or ears to hear God. So even though God's word is perfect, we are dependent upon the Holy Spirit working in us to hear God's word read and preached. We acknowledge with the psalmist that only "in your light do we see light" (Ps. 36:9) and must pray as Paul prayed for the church at Ephesus to have the "eyes of your hearts enlightened" (Eph. 1:18).]

Because we see but do not perceive and hear but do not understand, let us ask God the Spirit to enlighten our minds and quicken our hearts so that we might hear, believe, and obey his voice.

> Make your face shine upon your servant,
>   and teach me your statutes. (Ps. 119:135)

> Open my eyes, that I may behold
>   wondrous things out of your law. (Ps. 119:18)

The Proclamation of God's Word

[**Note:** As we learned in chapter 6, the principal means by which we see the glory of God in the face of Christ and witness the beatific vision until that time when we see God face-to-face is through the preaching of God's word. Just as Israel "saw" God at Mount Sinai by hearing God speak (Deut. 4:12), our desire to see Jesus (John 12:21) is met in hearing his voice through preaching (Rom. 10:14–17). Paul's rebuke of the Galatians describes "hearing with faith" as the public portrayal of Christ crucified (Gal. 3:1–2). To preach Christ is to show Christ. Not just a thin Christ of the cross alone, as fundamental as the cross is, but the whole Christ. Just as the Song of Solomon is a meticulous inventory of the beauties of the king and his bride, we must preach the whole Christ from the whole Bible just as we might examine every hue and brushstroke of a great painting. Our aim is for God's people to "behold the king in his beauty" (Isa. 33:17).]

♫

Song

[**Note:** Singing in response to hearing the word of God can vary widely according to the subject or theme of the sermon, such as acknowledgement, affirmation, dedication, resolution to action, and comfort through hope. There are many hymns and songs that express these responses with reference to the face of God and the face of Christ. Following are a few sample lyrics with such responses.]

Through God's word we have seen the King in his beauty, and we have heard his voice; therefore, let us be faithful to this heavenly vision by responding in song.

Here, O my Lord, I see thee face to face;
here would I touch and handle things unseen,

here grasp with firmer hand th'eternal grace,
and all my weariness upon thee lean.[1]

or

Arise, O God, and shine
in all thy saving might,
and prosper each design
to spread thy glorious light . . .

Send forth thy glorious pow'r,
that Gentiles all may see,
and earth present her store
in converts born to thee . . .[2]

or

The King there in his beauty
without a veil is seen;
it were a well-spent journey,
though sev'n deaths lay between

The bride eyes not her garment,
but her dear bride-groom's face;
I will not gaze at glory,
but on my King of grace . . .[3]

1   Horatius Bonar, "Here, O My Lord, I See Thee Face to Face," *Trinity Hymnal*, rev. ed. (Atlanta: Great Commission Publications, 1997), no. 378.
2   William Hurn, "Arise, O God, and Shine," *Trinity Hymnal*, rev. ed. (Atlanta: Great Commission Publications, 1997), no. 442.
3   Samuel Rutherford and Anne R. Cousin, "The Sands of Time Are Sinking," *Trinity Hymnal*, rev. ed. (Atlanta: Great Commission Publications, 1997), no. 546.

Benediction

[**Note:** Great drama does not sputter or fade at the end but climaxes. It is easy for pastors and other worship leaders to be "out of gas" as worship concludes. Yet if the beatific vision is the greatest good, then the Aaronic blessing can serve as the climactic conclusion of worship. As explained in chapter 6, the benediction is not a prayer but a pronouncement. Therefore, an appropriate exhortation can precede the benediction so that God's people experience more fully the glory and wonder of God's benevolence in the benediction. As you exhort, look at the faces of the congregation and pause before exercising the privilege to be God's instrument to bless them.]

Lift up your eyes to receive the blessing of the Lord.

> The Lord bless you and keep you;
> the Lord make his face to shine upon you and be gracious
>   to you;
> the Lord lift up his countenance upon you and give you
>   peace. (Num. 6:24–26)

Doxology

[**Note:** Imagine a great love story leading up to a perfectly timed wedding proposal to which the response is, "Sure, why not?" There wouldn't be much romance in that relationship, would there? A doxology is a human response to God's benediction and should be an exuberant, "I do!" The doxology can be exclaimed by the minister on behalf of the people or by the people, in either word or song. The most exuberant doxology comes without instructions, but as a spontaneous eruption of praise. If offered in song, let the instrument(s) be the exhortation. If offered in word, the following exhortation from Psalm 103:2 is suitable.]

Let us "Bless the Lord, O my soul, and forget not all his benefits . . ."

He who is the blessed and only Sovereign, the King of kings and Lord of lords, who alone has immortality, who dwells in unapproachable light, whom no one has ever seen or can see. To him be honor and eternal dominion. Amen. (1 Tim. 6:15–16)

Charge

[**Note:** Just as God has shone his face on his people that he might be known to them, so God's people are to reflect the shining face of God outwardly to the world. Followers of Christ are to be doers of God's word, not just hearers (James 1:22). As Psalm 67:1–3 makes clear, God's gracious gaze revealed to his people should lead to him being made known in the world. Therefore, it is fitting that the last word of worship is a charge to the people, having given God glory in worship, to now glorify him in the world.]

Brothers and sisters upon whom the face of God shines in and through his beloved Son, go into the world so that God's gracious gaze may shine in the world.

> May God be gracious to us and bless us
>   and make his face to shine upon us, *Selah*
> that your way may be known on earth,
>   your saving power among all nations.
> Let the peoples praise you, O God;
>   let all the peoples praise you! (Ps. 67:1–3)

General Index

Aaron, 9, 17, 28, 35, 37, 72,
140–41, 147. *See also* Aaronic
blessing
Aaronic blessing, 3, 5, 8, 9, 32–34,
51–52, 53, 54, 56, 60, 67, 83,
87, 98, 104, 113, 126, 138,
175; and the Aaronic role of
priestly benediction, 75–76; as
the divine response to Israel's
consecration, 32; God's blessing will "keep" and "guard,"
34–35; and God's protection,
37; immediate context of in
the book of Numbers, 30–32;
progression of, 34; second line
of (graciousness to his people),
39–41, 46; third element of
(peace), 46–48. *See also* Aaronic blessing as libretto
Aaronic blessing as libretto, 146–47;
and assurance, 150; and benediction, 151–52; and confession, 148–49; and intercession,
151; and invocation, 147–48;
and praise, 148; and supplication, 150; and thanksgiving,
150–51

Abel, 13
Abraham, 18, 27–29
Abram, 13, 164
accessibility, 138–39
Adam, 2, 22–23, 31, 48, 87, 114
Anabaptists, 153

Baal, 37
Babel, 13
Babylon, 60
baca (weeping), 97
baptism, Christian, 103
Barclay, John, 73, 132–33
benediction(s): choosing, 161–63;
ministry of, 152–63
Berridge, John, 96
Berry, Wendell, 111
"Be Still, My Soul" (von Schlegel),
97
biblical metaphors, 40
Bonhoeffer, Dietrich, 129–31
Book of Common Prayer, 148

Cain, 11–13; fratricide of, 116
Calvin, John, 83–84; on the Psalms
as "an anatomy of all Parts of
the Soul," 44

prayer, 143–44; and the "exile of
    public prayer," 143
Prescott, Catherine, 2
priesthood (a better priesthood),
    51–54
prophets, Spirit-inspired, 84–85
Protestant Reformation and Re-
    formers, 128, 153
protoevangelium, 11

Rebekah, 13
righteousness (greater righteous-
    ness), 129–33; of the kingdom
    of heaven, 131
"Ripple" (Grateful Dead), 56
Robin, Christopher, 104

Sabbath, the, obligations of for
    justice and mercy, 118
sanctuary, 29; Edenic sanctuary, 31
Sande, Ken, on gospel-centered
    peacemaking, 124n6
"Sands of Time Are Sinking, The"
    (Cousin), 173–74
Sasse, Ben, 122–23
Saving Private Ryan (1998), 8
Scripture: divine reading of,
    56–57n10; role of in worship,
    143
Second Helvetic Confession,
    153–55
Sermon on the Mount, 130
Seth, 50
Shalom ("peace"), 46–47, 148;
    and biblical laws of restitu-
    tion, 47; covenantal nature
    of, 47, 48; as the fruit of
    salvation, 47; and God's
    presence, 48–49; wholeness
    of, 47

sin, 89; confession of, 148–49; and
    grief, 90–91; interpersonal
    sins, 30
Spielberg, Steven, 8
"Stairway to Heaven" (Led Zep-
    pelin), 107
Steele, Anne, 103

temptation, liberation from, 55
theophanies, 48
"Thou Lovely Source of True De-
    light" (Steele), 103
Till We Have Faces (Lewis), 1–2,
    106, 169–70
triune God, unity of, 126–27

von Schlegel, Katharina, 97
Voyage of the Dawn Treader, The
    (Lewis), 93–95

Way to Pray, A (Henry), 145–46
Wesley, Charles, 16
Westminster Shorter Catechism, 89
*Why We Hate Each Other—and
    How to Heal* (Sasse), 122
Willimon, William, 158–59
worship, 138; basic shape of,
    139–40; community worship,
    160; contemporary worship,
    142–43; God as the royal audi-
    ence in our worship, 141–42;
    maintaining healthy worship,
    145–46; nonparticipatory wor-
    ship, 143; participatory wor-
    ship, 143; and prayer, 143–44;
    proper conclusion to, 164–65;
    role of Scripture in, 143; set-
    ting the table for, 138–46;
    two-phase worship, 144–45.
    See also worship, order of

Scripture Index